BRANCH LINES AROUND PLYMOUTH

Vic Mitchell and Keith Smith

Middleton Press

Cover picture: The Southern Railway's Turnchapel branch was worked by a class O2 0-4-4T no. 200 on 5th August 1928. The 7.50pm departure from Plymouth Friary is standing at Lucas Terrace Halt, with Friary Shed in the background. (H.C.Casserley)

First Published 1997
Reprinted July 2004

ISBN 1 873793 98 7

© *Middleton Press, 1997*

Design   Deborah Esher
Typesetting   Barbara Mitchell

Published by
               Middleton Press
               Easebourne Lane
               Midhurst, West Sussex
               GU29 9AZ
Tel: 01730 813169
Fax: 01730 812601
Email: info@middletonpress.co.uk
www.middletonpress.co.uk

Printed & bound by MPG Books, Bodmin

CONTENTS

1. **Western Plymouth**
   - Millbay District — 1-15
   - Stonehouse Pool Branch — 16-19
   - Admiralty Dockyard, Devonport — 20-27
2. **Eastern Plymouth**
   - Lee Moor Tramway — 28-40

Friary District — 41- 60
Sutton Harbour Branch — 61- 68
Cattewater Branch — 69- 84
Turnchapel Branch — 85- 99
Yealmpton Branch — 100-120

ACKNOWLEDGEMENTS

In addition to those mentioned in the photographic credits, we have received assistance from P.G.Barnes, G.Croughton, D.Cullum, K.Horne, N.Langridge, Mr D. and Dr S.Salter and E.Youldon. To all these, and in particular our wives, we express our sincere gratitude for their help.

INDEX

20	Admiralty Dockyard, Devonport	3	Millbay
107	Billacombe	9	Millbay Docks
111	Brixton Road	87	Oreston
69	Cattewater Branch	85	Plymstock (south side)
56	Cattewater Junction	100	Plymstock (north side)
1	Cornwall Junction	113	Steer Point
110	Elburton Cross	16	Stonehouse Pool Branch
41	Friary	61	Sutton Harbour Branch
50	Friary Shed	92	Turnchapel
38	Laira Junction	80	Victoria Wharf
28	Lee Moor Tramway	114	Yealmpton
53	Lucas Terrace Halt		

MAPS

I	Western Plymouth 1923		XVI	Friary Shed 25 ins 1933
II	Eastern Plymouth 1922		XVII	Sutton Harbour 25 ins 1914
III	Western Plymouth Street plan 1920s		XVIII	Laira Wharf 25 ins 1933
IV	Millbay Branch 6 ins 1938		XIX	Cattedown Wharves 25 ins 1914
V	Cornwall Junction 25 ins 1914		XX	Victoria Wharves 25 ins 1914
VI	Millbay 25 ins 1914		XXI	Plymstock 25 ins 1914
VII	Millbay Docks 25 ins 1914		XXII	Oreston 25 ins 1914
VIII	Devonport 25 ins 1934		XXIII	Turnchapel 25 ins 1914
IX	Stonehouse Pool 25 ins 1907		XXIV	Yealmpton Branch 1 ins 1946
X	Admiralty Dockyard 17 ins 1912		XXV	Billacombe 25 ins 1933
XI	Admiralty Dockyard route diagram		XXVI	Elburton Cross 25 ins 1933
XII	Eastern Plymouth street plan 1920s		XXVII	Brixton Road 25 ins 1933
XIII	Laira Wharf 25 ins 1914		XXVIII	Steer Point 25 ins 1913
XIV	Laira Junction 25 ins 1933		XXIX	Yealmpton 25 ins 1906
XV	Friary to Turnchapel 6 ins 1938			

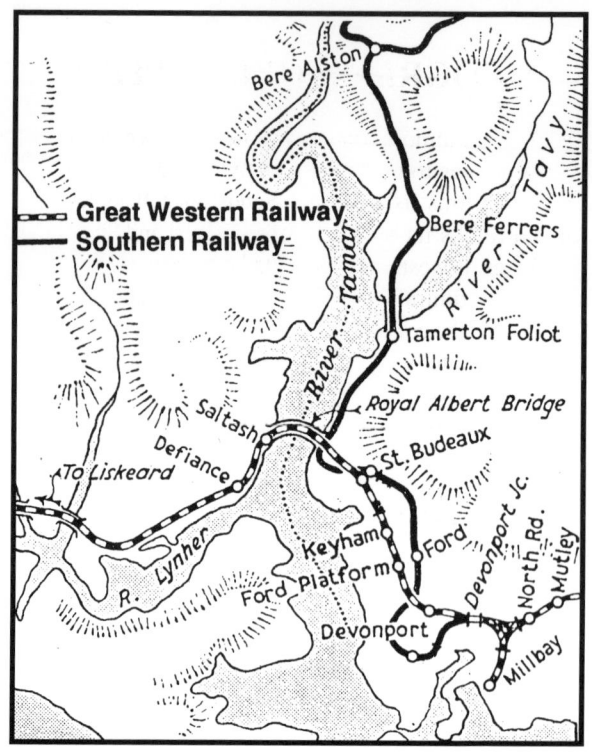

I Map of the passenger routes in Western Plymouth in 1923. (Railway Magazine)

II Map of the lines of Eastern Plymouth in 1922. (Railway Magazine)

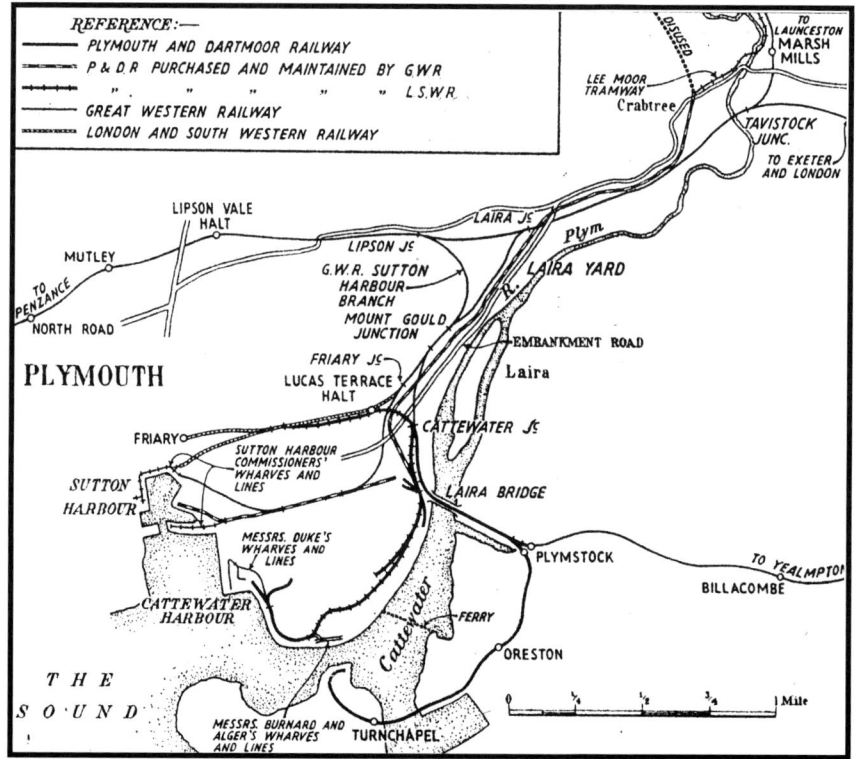

GEOGRAPHICAL SETTING

Plymouth is situated on an almost square area of elevated land which slopes towards the waterfronts. The River Plym forms its eastern boundary, while The Sound flanks its southern edge and the River Tamar forms its western limit. The old established Devonport Admiralty Dockyard is on this side, while most of the commercial docks are to the south, separated into two groups by the high ground of Plymouth Hoe.

Much of the southern area is formed of Limestone, which was of economic importance in bygone days, but most of Plymouth is on Red Sandstones. It achieved city status in 1914, when Devonport and Stonehouse were included within its boundary.

The maps herein are to the scale of 25 ins to 1 mile, unless otherwise indicated. North is at the top of the maps, except where an arrow is included.

HISTORICAL BACKGROUND

Plymouth & Dartmoor Railway

This was the first railway in the area and was authorised under an Act of 2nd July 1819. Further Acts in 1820 and 1821 gave a total mileage of 25½. The main purpose of this 4 ft 6 ins gauge line was the conveyance of timber, lime and other building materials from Plymouth to a new prison under construction near Princetown. It was to house prisoners from the Napoleonic Wars. The route from Sutton Pool to King's Tor was opened on 26th September 1823 and was horse-worked.

The line fell into disuse in the 1840s, the northern part eventually becoming part of the Princetown branch. The Lee Moor Tramway on Dartmoor was connected to a branch of the southern section in 1856 for the conveyance of china clay, traffic being destined to Laira Wharf, below Laira Bridge. The line remained in use (for gravel, but still horse operated) south to Maddocks Concrete Works at the south end of Laira Yard until October 1960, the southern section to Cattewater Harbour having closed in 1947.

Great Western Railway

Its predecessor in the area was the South Devon Railway, which opened a broad gauge (7 ft 0¼ ins) line from Totnes to Plymouth (Laira Green) on 5th May 1848. The route was extended from this temporary terminus to a new one at Millbay on 2nd April 1849.

The Cornwall Railway came into use in 1859 and also used Millbay as its terminus. The SDR and the CR both became part of the GWR, the former in 1878 and the latter in 1889, although both had been worked by the GWR for some years previously.

The SDR gained access to Sutton Pool (later Harbour) by laying an additional rail alongside those of the P&DR south of Laira Junction in 1851. Dual gauge was in place until 1869, when two parallel tracks were brought into use.

The broad gauge lines of the area received an additional rail to accommodate standard gauge trains from 17th May 1876. Broad gauge traffic ceased on 20th May 1892.

The GWR became the Western Region of British Railways upon nationalisation in 1948.

London & South Western Railway

This ambitious company had long had Plymouth as its goal. Its line from Okehampton to Lydford opened on 12th October 1874 and its trains continued to Plymouth via the GWR-operated Launceston-Tavistock-Plymouth route, completed in 1859-65. The LSWR trains terminated at their impressive new station in Devonport.

Seeking a route not controlled by their rival, the LSWR encouraged the Plymouth, Devonport & South Western Junction Railway to build a line from Lydford to Devonport via

Bere Alston. From 2nd June 1890, LSWR trains from London were able to enter their Devonport station from the opposite direction. As the trains were no longer passing through Plymouth, they built a new terminus at Plymouth Friary, this coming into use on 1st July 1891.

The LSWR became part of the Southern Railway in 1923, which in turn formed the Southern Region of British Railways in 1948. Those lines in the Plymouth area were transferred to the Western Region in 1958.

Turnchapel Branch

The LSWR used the almost moribund Plymouth & Dartmoor Railway to obtain an Act to construct a line to Turnchapel. The Act was passed on 2nd August 1883 and the line to Plymstock was opened on 5th September 1892. The extension to Turnchapel Wharf followed on 1st January 1897, passenger services to Turnchapel commencing on 1st July of that year.

Passenger trains were withdrawn from the branch on 10th September 1951 and goods services ceased on 30th October 1961. There had been temporary cessation of passenger services between 14th January and 2nd July 1951, due to a coal shortage, and this resulted in most travellers finding other means of transport.

Yealmpton Branch

The South Hams Railway was promoted in 1888 by the Plymouth & Dartmoor Railway, the company formed in 1819 and used in the 1870s to act as an agent for the LSWR in its expansion in the area. An Act in 1892 transferred the powers obtained by the PDR for the construction of a line from Plymstock to Yealmpton to the GWR. The branch opened on 17th January 1898.

Passenger services were withdrawn on 7th July 1930, but restored on 3rd November 1941 at a time when the enemy aerial bombardment of Plymouth was so severe that a high proportion of its residents abandoned the city each night. Final withdrawal came on 7th October 1947, but freight traffic continued until 29th February 1960, when the service was cut back to Plymstock.

PASSENGER SERVICES

Turnchapel Branch

Eight return trips (weekdays only) were provided at first but this was soon reduced to seven. The table below reveals the good service frequency that was provided following the introduction of railmotor services in 1905.

	Weekdays	Sundays
1904	12	0
1905	18	0
1920	20	0
1930	26	14
1940	19	8
1950	19	0

Yealmpton Branch

The initial service was one of five return journeys, weekdays only, to and from Millbay. There were additional journeys by railmotors between Plymstock and Saltash from 1904, eleven on weekdays and eight on Sundays.

The table gives an indication of the early variation and later stability.

	Weekdays	Sundays
1902	9	2
1904	6	6
1908	9	4
1920	7	0
1930	8	0
1942	8	0

During the 1941-47 revival period, trains ran to and from Plymouth Friary.

Timetables for Plymouth and Turnchapel (July 1908, July 1929), Plymouth and Yealmpton (July 1899, October 1905, July 1929).

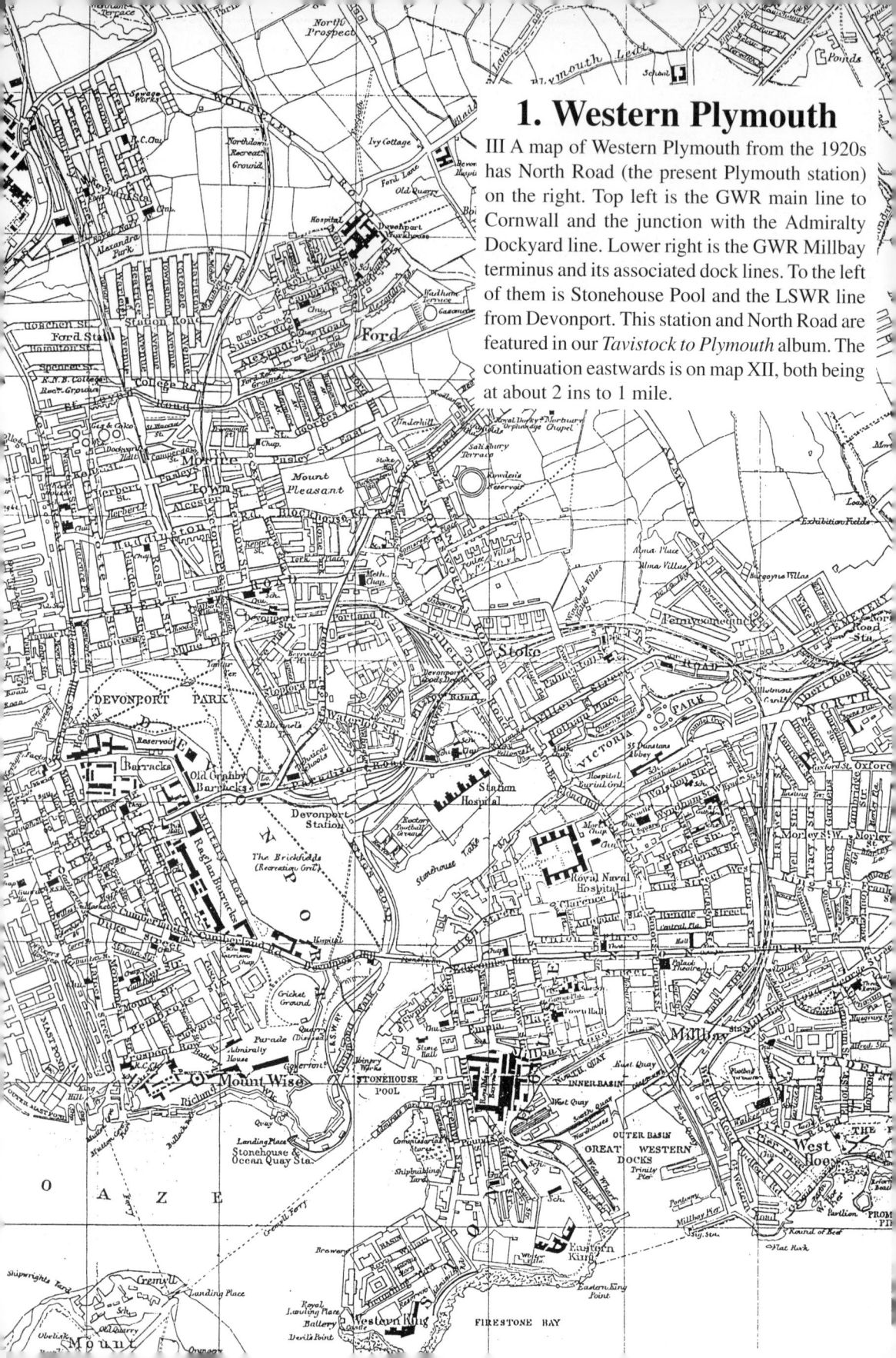

1. Western Plymouth

III A map of Western Plymouth from the 1920s has North Road (the present Plymouth station) on the right. Top left is the GWR main line to Cornwall and the junction with the Admiralty Dockyard line. Lower right is the GWR Millbay terminus and its associated dock lines. To the left of them is Stonehouse Pool and the LSWR line from Devonport. This station and North Road are featured in our *Tavistock to Plymouth* album. The continuation eastwards is on map XII, both being at about 2 ins to 1 mile.

IV The 1938 edition at 6 ins to 1 mile has North Road station top right, while top left is Devonport Junction, the point of divergence of the GWR and SR routes. Millbay station is below centre.

MILLBAY DISTRICT
CORNWALL JUNCTION

1. Cornwall Junction was at the southern end of the triangular junction shown on the maps and is beyond the left border of this 1959 photograph. In the distance is West Junction. The lines in the foreground led to a turntable from 1913 to 1966. (A.E.Bennett)

V. Published in 1914, this map fails to include the sidings and turntable shown on map IV, but it does mark the Belmont Street engine sheds and the Harwell Street carriage shed. The approach to Millbay is at the bottom and continues at the top of the next map. The northern part of the triangle came into use on 17th May 1876 and was known as the "Cornwall Loop". Cornwall Junction Box (above centre) closed on 26th November 1960 but Belmont Diesel Depot was in use until 4th October 1964. ⟶

2. This northward view of the Millbay sheds was taken before the carriage shed was built. The line to Millbay is slightly elevated on the right and descended at 1 in 61 to 65 to the station. (M.Dart coll.)

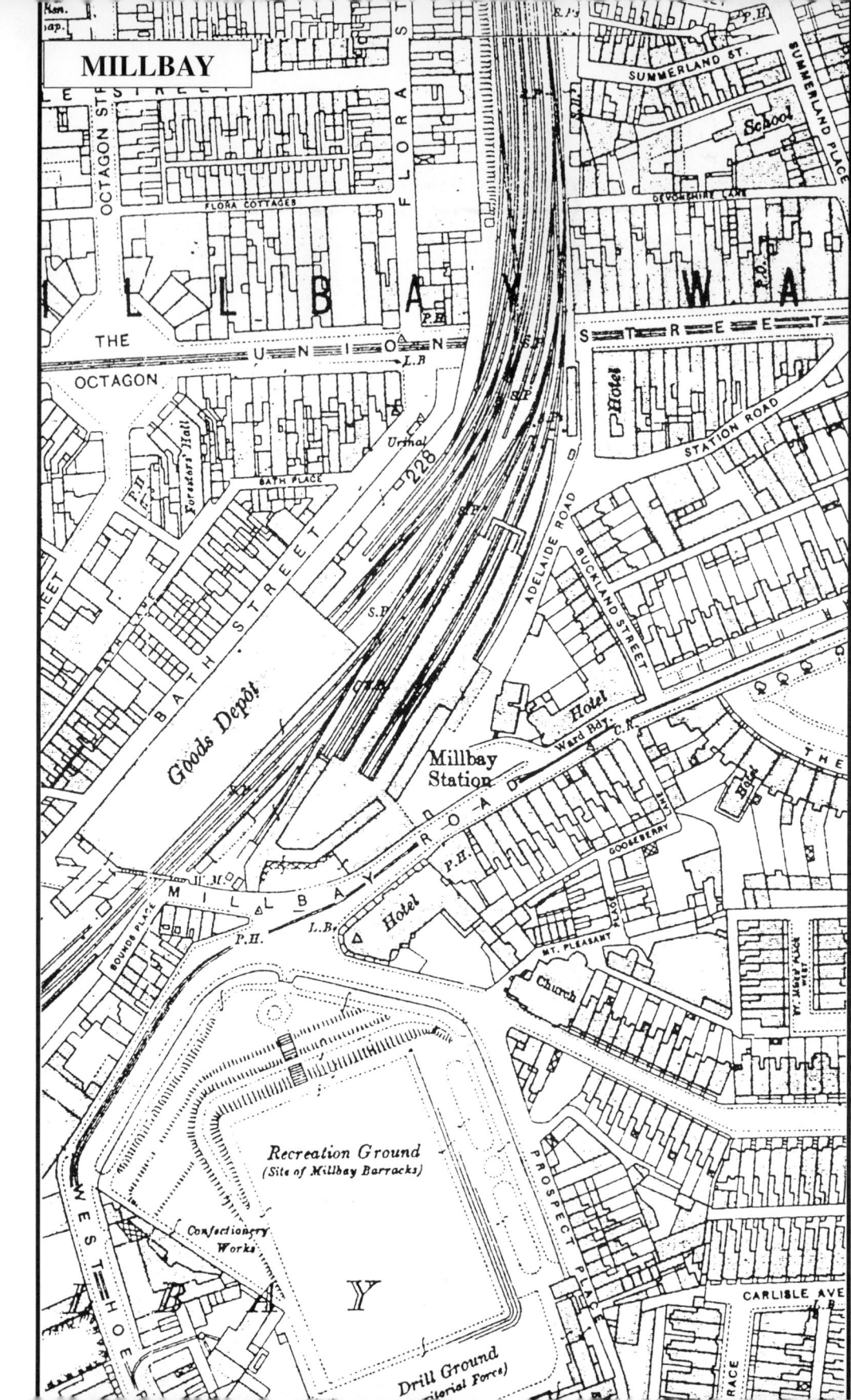

←

VI. A footbridge at the outer ends of the platforms was of benefit to passengers changing trains. Local services used platforms 1 and 4, while main line trains were allocated the centre two. The street tramway operated until 1936. Some of the arches adjacent to the Union Street bridge (above centre) were used as stables for GWR horses.

3. A northward view from Millbay Road shows one of two entrances for road traffic. The other was adjacent to the Continental Hotel, which stands in the background. The station was rebuilt in 1900, as seen. (M.Dart coll.)

4. A photograph taken from the hotel reveals the size of the station buildings and the covered carriageway. The standing cabs of yesterday produced a different form of pollution from those of today; an attendant cleaner was required very regularly. (M.Dart coll.)

5. We now have four pictures from 1959. Passenger services had ceased on 23rd April 1941, due to the severe bombing of the district. Looking north we see the dock lines on the left and the signal box in the left distance. This was in use from 1914 until 14th December 1969. (A.E.Bennett)

6. The station area was used for carriage storage after 1941; the platforms were removed and additional sidings provided during 1959. The DMU was hired for a Railway Enthusiasts Club railtour on 11th April of that year; it is seen again later on the Yealmpton line. (A.E.Bennett)

7. The west elevation is evident, as is the top of the spacious Duke of Cornwall Hotel (left), which is one of the few historic buildings (1862) to remain in the area. On the right is the fish dock and its two sidings. (A.E.Bennett)

8. The double track to Millbay Docks descends on a curve past the goods shed. The yard was recorded as having a 6-ton crane in 1938, while there was one of 25-ton capacity in the Docks. (A.E.Bennett)

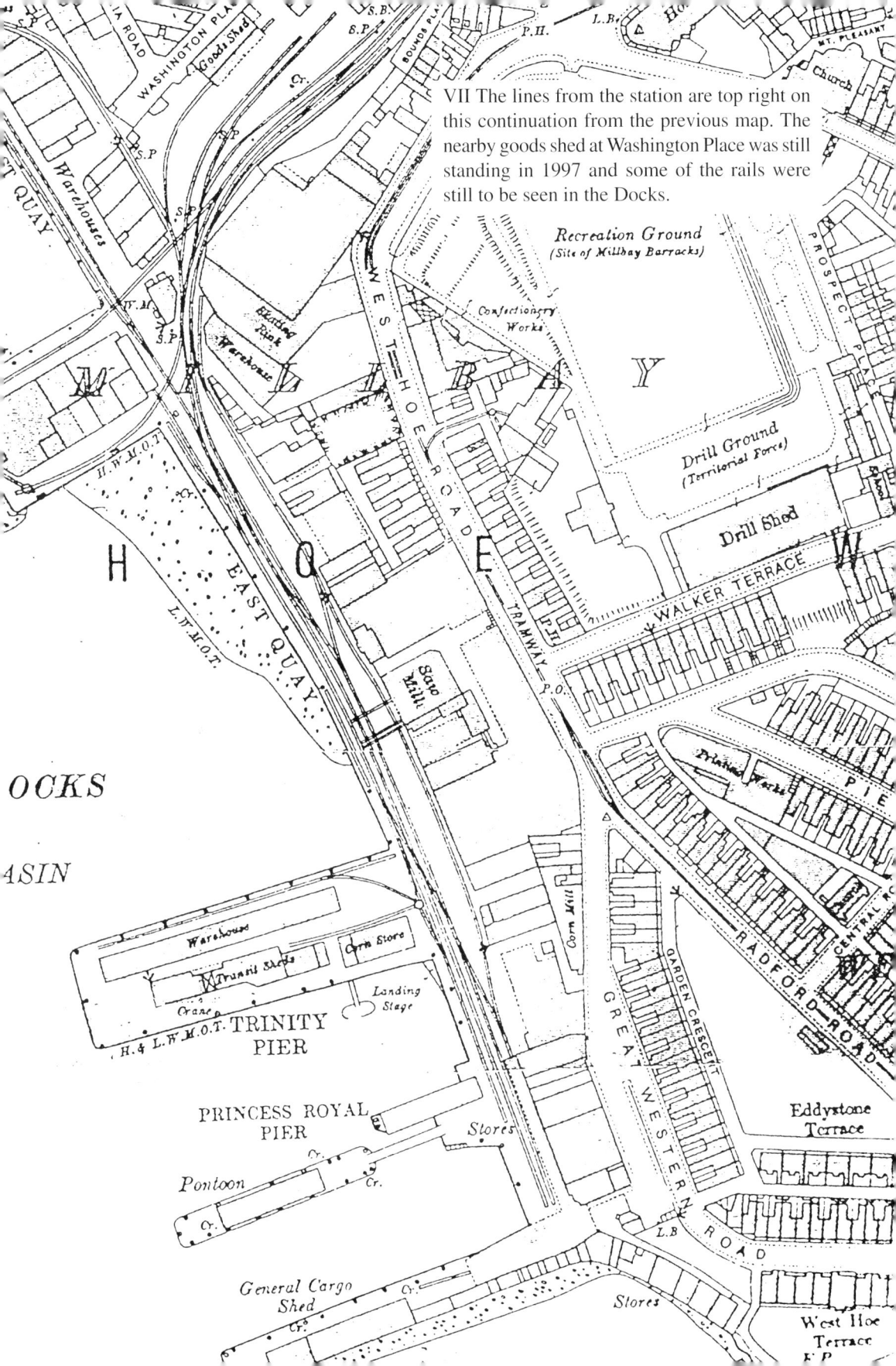

VII The lines from the station are top right on this continuation from the previous map. The nearby goods shed at Washington Place was still standing in 1997 and some of the rails were still to be seen in the Docks.

MILLBAY DOCKS

9. Class N 2-6-0 no. 31835 crosses Millbay Road with vans and cattle wagons as it leaves the Docks and passes the signal box, which was in use until 17th March 1968. The crossing is shown on the left of map VI. The footbridge on which the photographer is standing is on the right of picture no. 6. (M.Daly)

10. This scene near South Quay is typical of the dockside trackwork of the area. Ship repair was carried out in this vicinity - note the funnel parked on the right. The docks had become railway owned in 1874. (L.Crosier)

11. On the right is Trinity Pier, a pontoon and Millbay Pier; nearby is the Ocean Terminal for boat trains from Paddington. Passengers and mailbags were conveyed by small ships (tenders) to and from transatlantic liners waiting in Plymouth Sound from 1850 to 1963. The peak year for mail was 1949, when 437,295 bags were landed. (M.Dart coll.)

12. A passenger train stands on East Quay as tenders wait at the piers. The liners were passing to and from such places as Hamburg, Rotterdam, London, Southampton, Cherbourg, Le Havre and Liverpool. Almost 800 vessels called in 1930, but the figure had diminished to 93 in 1960. Passengers to London could save more than 24 hours by disembarking at this port-of-call. (M.Dart coll.)

13. There was no platform at East Quay and so passengers were provided with a series of steps, these being photographed in 1931. The LSWR provided the GWR with stiff competition in the 1904-06 period, London being reached within minutes of four hours. Complete boat trains were seldom required by the 1960s; a few coaches were taken to North Road and coupled to the next train for London. (British Rail)

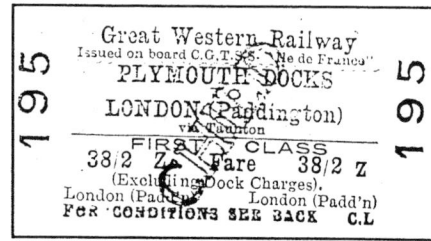

14. Shunting on East Quay in 1952 is no. 1361, one of a class of five 0-6-0STs built for this type of work in 1910 by the GWR. The shunters truck was a style peculiar to the GWR. (M.Dart coll.)

15. A 1961 photograph features the locomotive water tank and adjacent engine shed, which was called "Plymouth Dock" and which closed in about 1955. The section from North Road to the Docks closed completely on 30th June 1971. (R.S.Carpenter)

STONEHOUSE POOL BRANCH

VIII The SR Devonport station is featured in *Tavistock to Plymouth* (pictures 90-98) but its map is included herein as the branch commenced in the goods yard and passed under the goods shed in a tunnel. This is the 1934 edition.

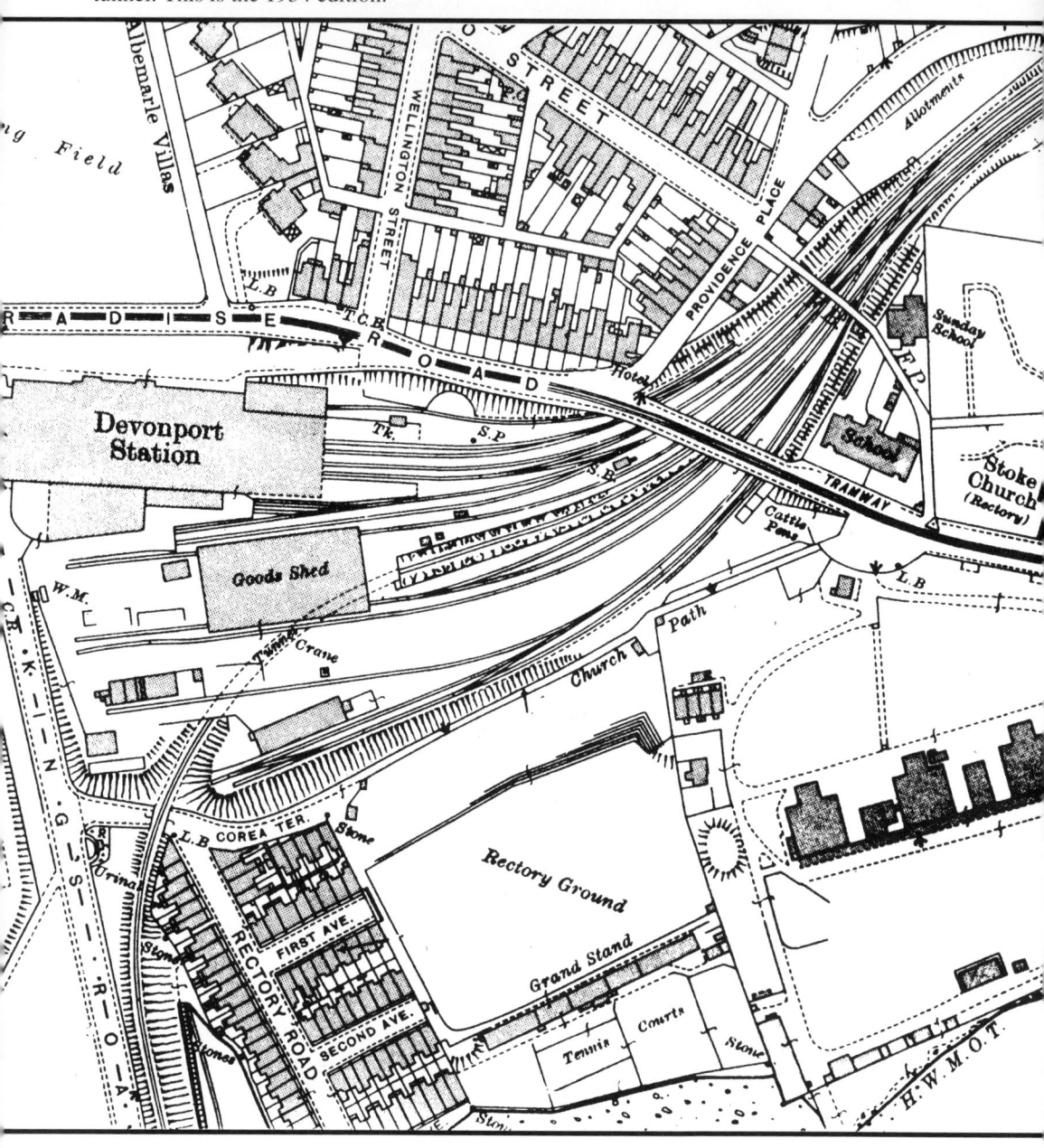

16. The southern portal of the tunnel and the bridge over Rectory Road was recorded from above the urinal shown on the map. The large building is the goods shed. (A.Jeffery)

17. The Plymouth Railway Circle arranged a trip down the branch to the former Ocean Quay station on 18th June 1966, the locomotive being no. D2177. It is approaching the bridge under the cross roads at the foot of Devonport Hill. This part of the route is now a public footpath. (M.J.Messenger)

18. A southward view includes the points at the approach to the terminus. The LSWR provided a competitive service for liner passengers to and from London, but the high-speed boat train disaster at Salisbury in 1906 tempered the race with the GWR thereafter. (H.Davies)

19. Ocean Quay was difficult to operate, being on a curve, but passengers were at least provided with a platform. The branch closed officially on 30th May 1970, although the last goods had been moved in June 1966. (M.Dart coll.)

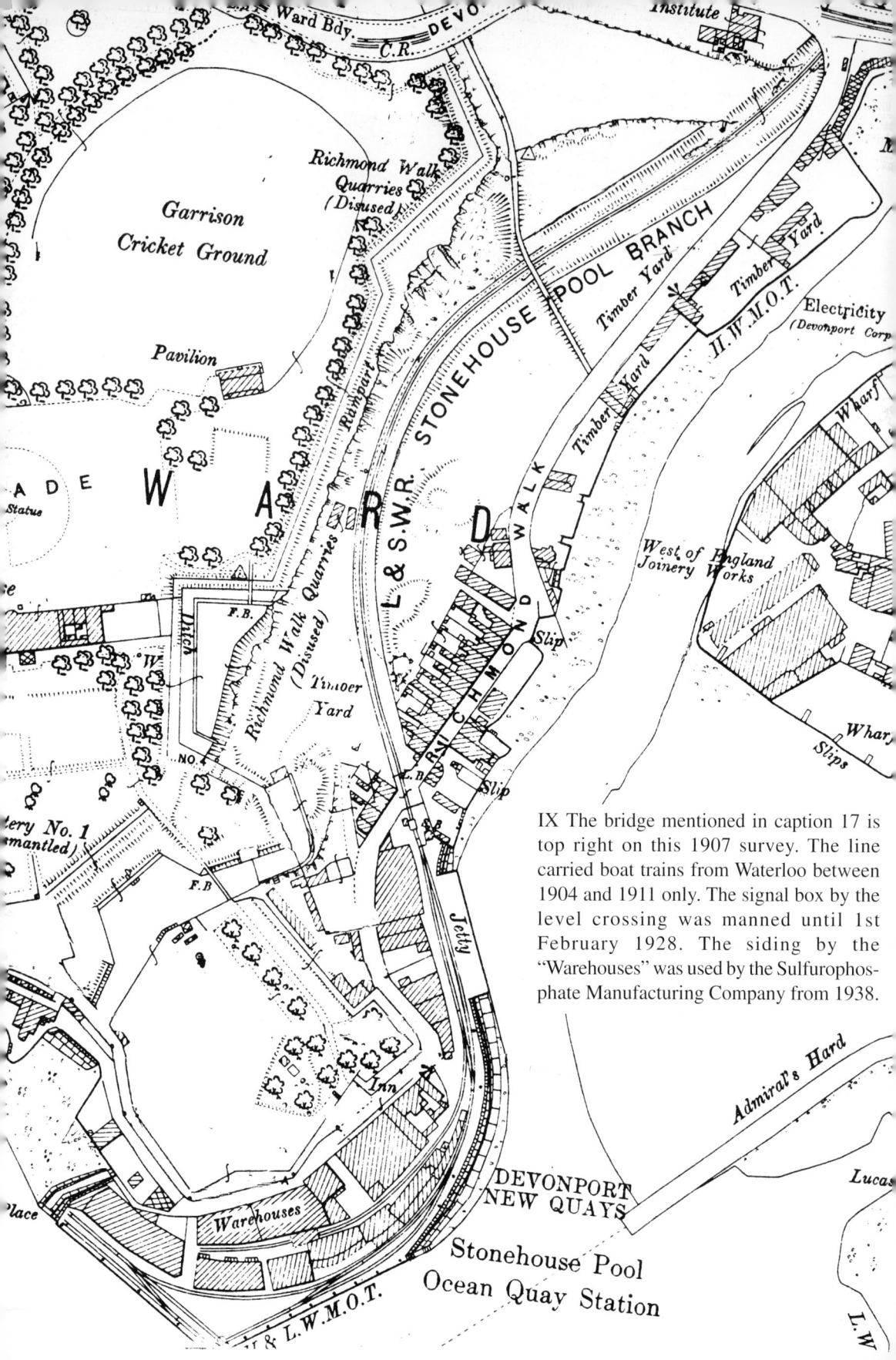

IX The bridge mentioned in caption 17 is top right on this 1907 survey. The line carried boat trains from Waterloo between 1904 and 1911 only. The signal box by the level crossing was manned until 1st February 1928. The siding by the "Warehouses" was used by the Sulfurophosphate Manufacturing Company from 1938.

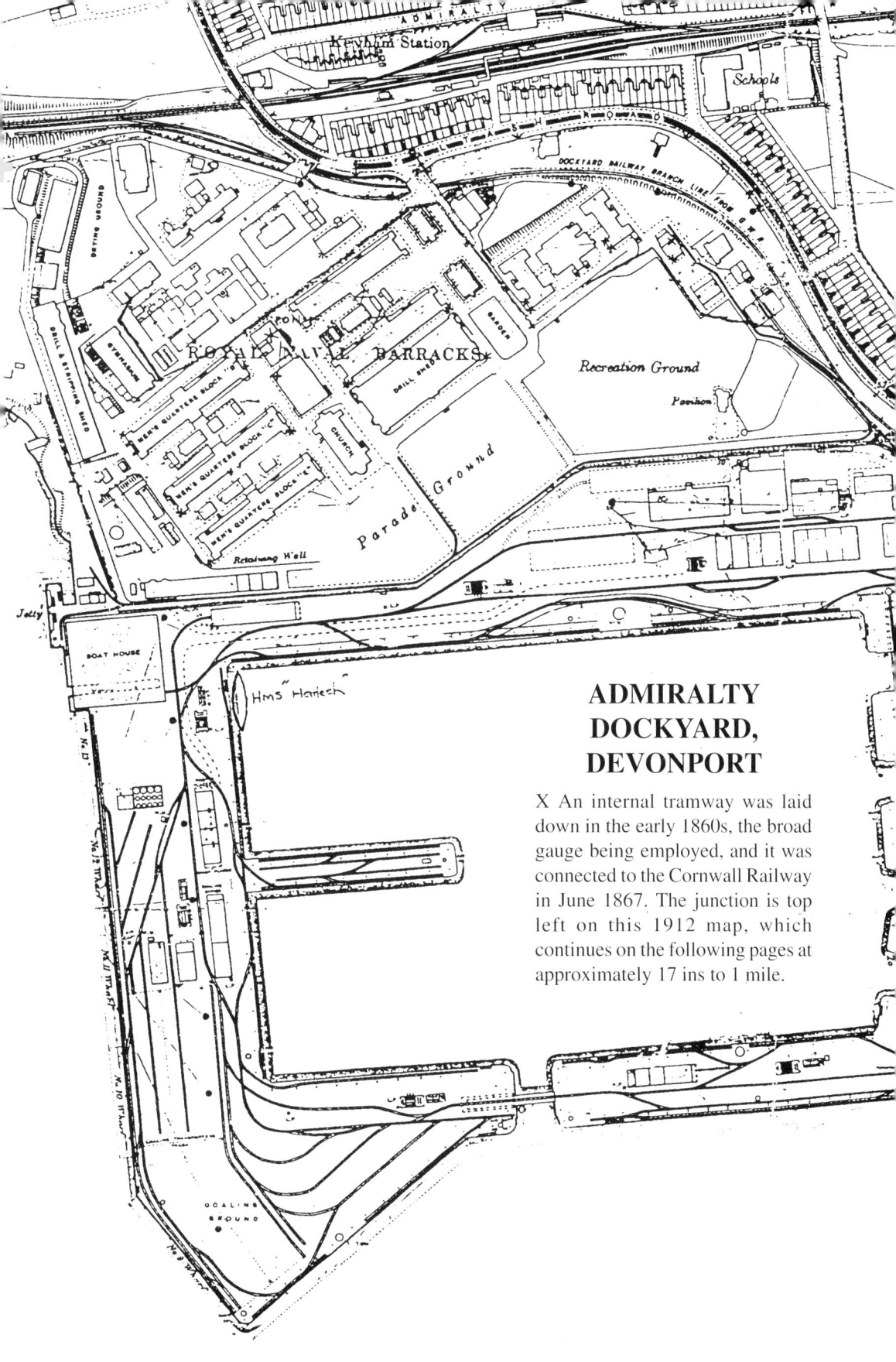

ADMIRALTY DOCKYARD, DEVONPORT

X An internal tramway was laid down in the early 1860s, the broad gauge being employed, and it was connected to the Cornwall Railway in June 1867. The junction is top left on this 1912 map, which continues on the following pages at approximately 17 ins to 1 mile.

20. A northward view of Keyham Junction has the Dockyard lines on the left and Weston Mill Viaduct in the background. There had been a facing connection from the up line (right) until 1956. The loop line on the extreme left was removed in 1973.
(L.Crosier/M.Dart)

21. At the head of a passenger train in South Yard on 25th May 1951 is no. 13, a locomotive built by Andrew Barclay & Co in 1915. The passenger service ran every half hour through the working day, and comprised wooden bodies on second-hand four-wheel goods rolling stock chassis. There were no less than five different classes of accommodation. (Plymouth Naval Base Museum)

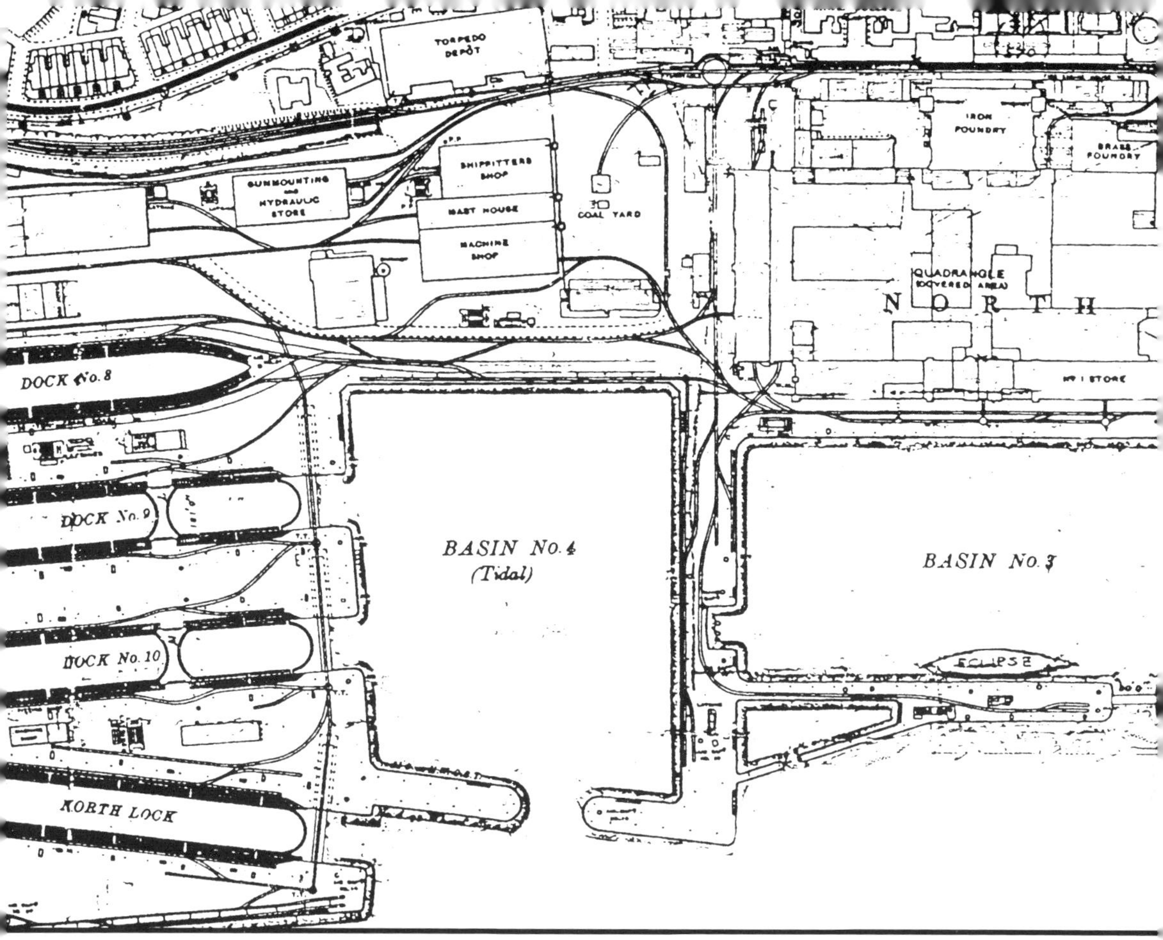

22. Photographed in about 1948, outside Central Offices in North Yard, this is no. 1, built in 1899 by Hawthorn Leslie & Co. The Royal Crest was attached when this engine hauled King Edward VII and Queen Alexandra in the Dockyard train on 8th March 1902. (Plymouth Naval Base Museum)

23. A Hibberd Planet diesel was recorded at the head of the passenger train at the North Yard terminus, in the early 1960s. Note the steps on the carriages, as there were no platforms at the stopping places. (P.Burkhalter coll.)

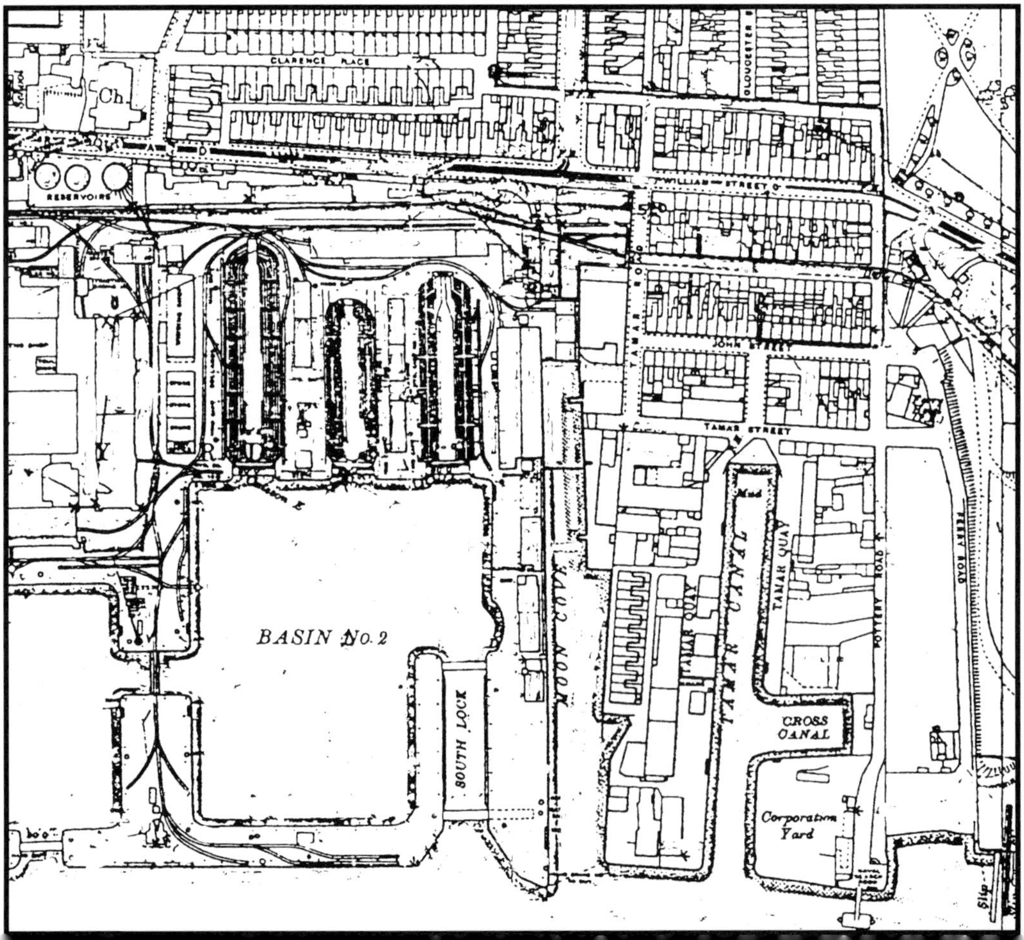

24. Hibberd Planet diesel (Yard no. 4860) was pictured just after emerging from the tunnel (to be glimpsed to the left of the cab) on the last day of rail traffic through to the South Yard on 10th November 1982. Also on the left is the Dockyard clock-tower which stands at the entrance to Albert Gate.
(P.Burkhalter coll.)

25. In the Exchange Sidings on 22nd June 1992 is a rake of VAA covered wagons being delivered by no. 37670. The chimney in the background is that which formerly served the furnaces of the Dockyard Foundry.
(P.Burkhalter)

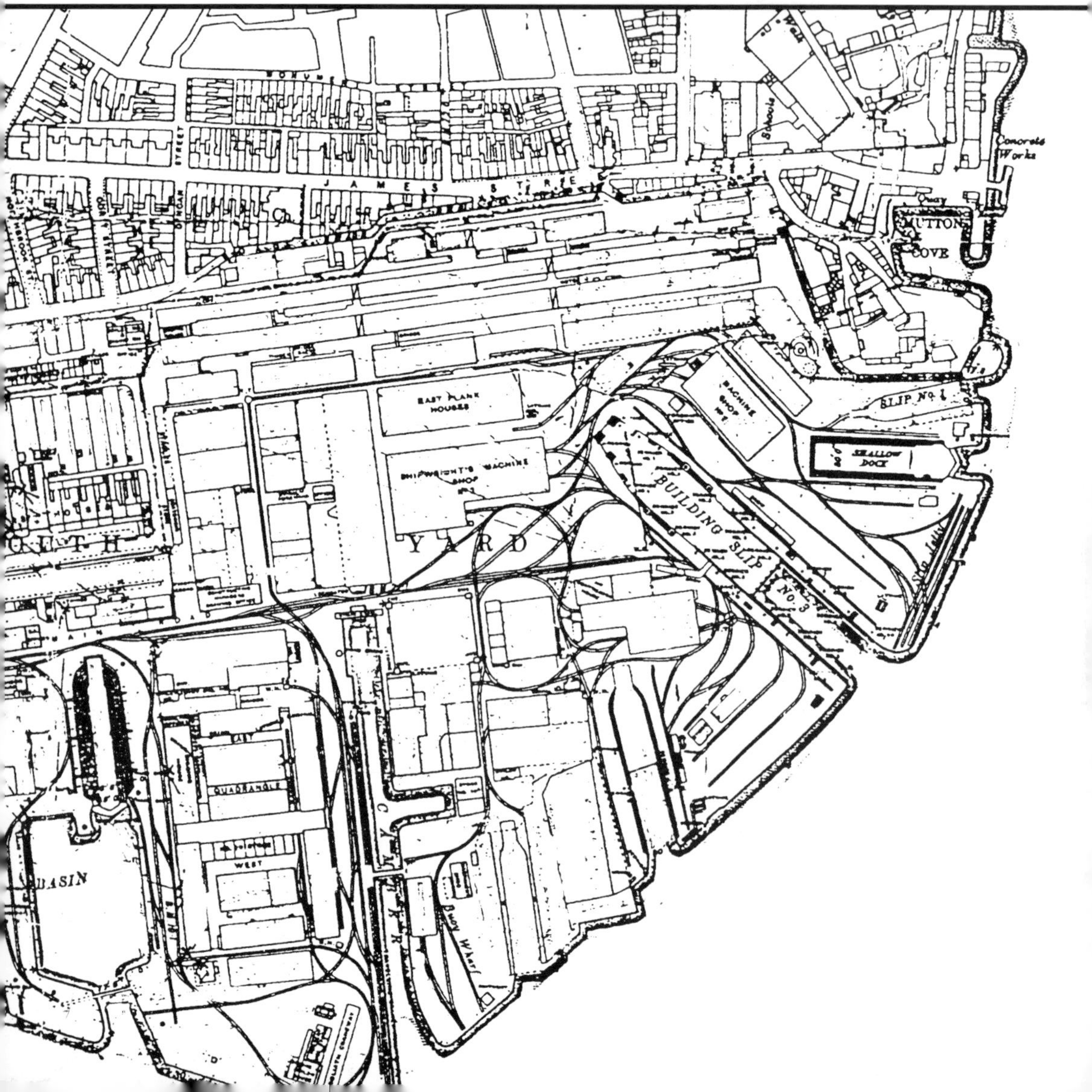

26. The Dockyard owners, Devonport Management Ltd., undertake rolling stock refurbishment, and here no. 08645 stands by the stop board at the north end of the exchange sidings ready to depart with a rake of HST coaches for which the barrier coach is required. Curving away in the distance in February 1995 is the 700 yard branch up a 1 in 70 gradient to Keyham Junction. (P.Burkhalter)

Diagram to show the two tunnels and six stopping places for passenger trains. This service ceased on 13th May 1966. (Railway Magazine)

27. Regular freight service ceased in about 1982 but occasional traffic necessitated the retention of two shunting locomotives. MOD Drewrys nos 249 and 230 were recorded in February 1995, when they were both 50 years old. (P.Burkhalter)

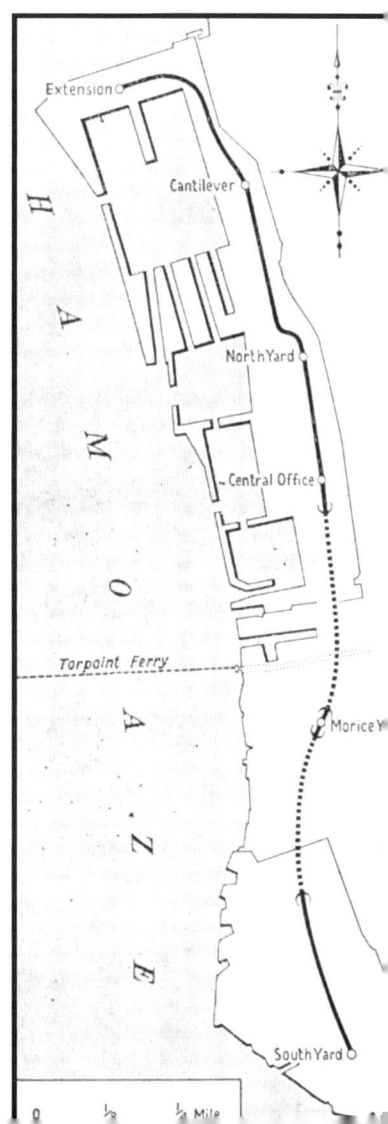

2. Eastern Plymouth

LEE MOOR TRAMWAY

XII While this street plan (continued from III) does not show the railway system comprehensively, it does help to relate the detailed maps that follow to one another.

28. The Plymouth & Dartmoor Railway was widely known as the Lee Moor Tramway in its latter years. Its southern terminus was at Laira Wharf, downstream from Laira Bridge and close to the Plymouth Corporation Electricity Works. The picture is from the 1930s. (M.Dart coll.)

31. Evident here is the very light rail section used on the tramway and the linkage to the motive power. Locomotives were employed on the middle level near the works and drying plants. (A.Bray/M.Dart)

32. The loading of a ship with bulk clay was very labour intensive. Its conveyance by sea during World War II was restricted and the wharf ceased to be used altogether in 1947. (A.Bray/M.Dart)

29. A view across Cattewater Harbour has the LSWR Cattewater Branch in the foreground with a ship being loaded with Lee Moor china clay. Breakwater Quarry is in the background. (ECC coll.)

30. Bulk clay is being unloaded while we have the opportunity to examine the simple 4 ft 6 ins gauge wagons. Dumb buffers sufficed but three sets of couplings were considered desirable on the rope worked inclines. (A.Bray/M.Dart)

33. Lump clay was transported in casks. Loading required less labour and was much cleaner. This northward view from the late 1930s has the SR on the left and Laira Bridge in the background. (A.Bray/M.Dart)

34. A northward panorama from Laira Bridge Road has the Turnchapel branch on the embankment on the right, the Cattewater branch close to it and Cattewater Junction signals in the background. The wagons of clay are about to pass under the road to reach Laira Wharf. (ECC coll.)

XIII From left to right at the top of this 1914 map - Sutton Harbour branch, Lee Moor Tramway, the Cattewater branch and the Turnchapel branch. The LMT appears to join the LSWR to pass under the road bridge; it then leaves it to reach Laira Wharf. The changes by 1933 can be seen in map XVIII and picture no. 69. Near the crane is Northney Siding; this was connected to the siding to the east of it during World War I to increase operational flexibility.

Plough Works

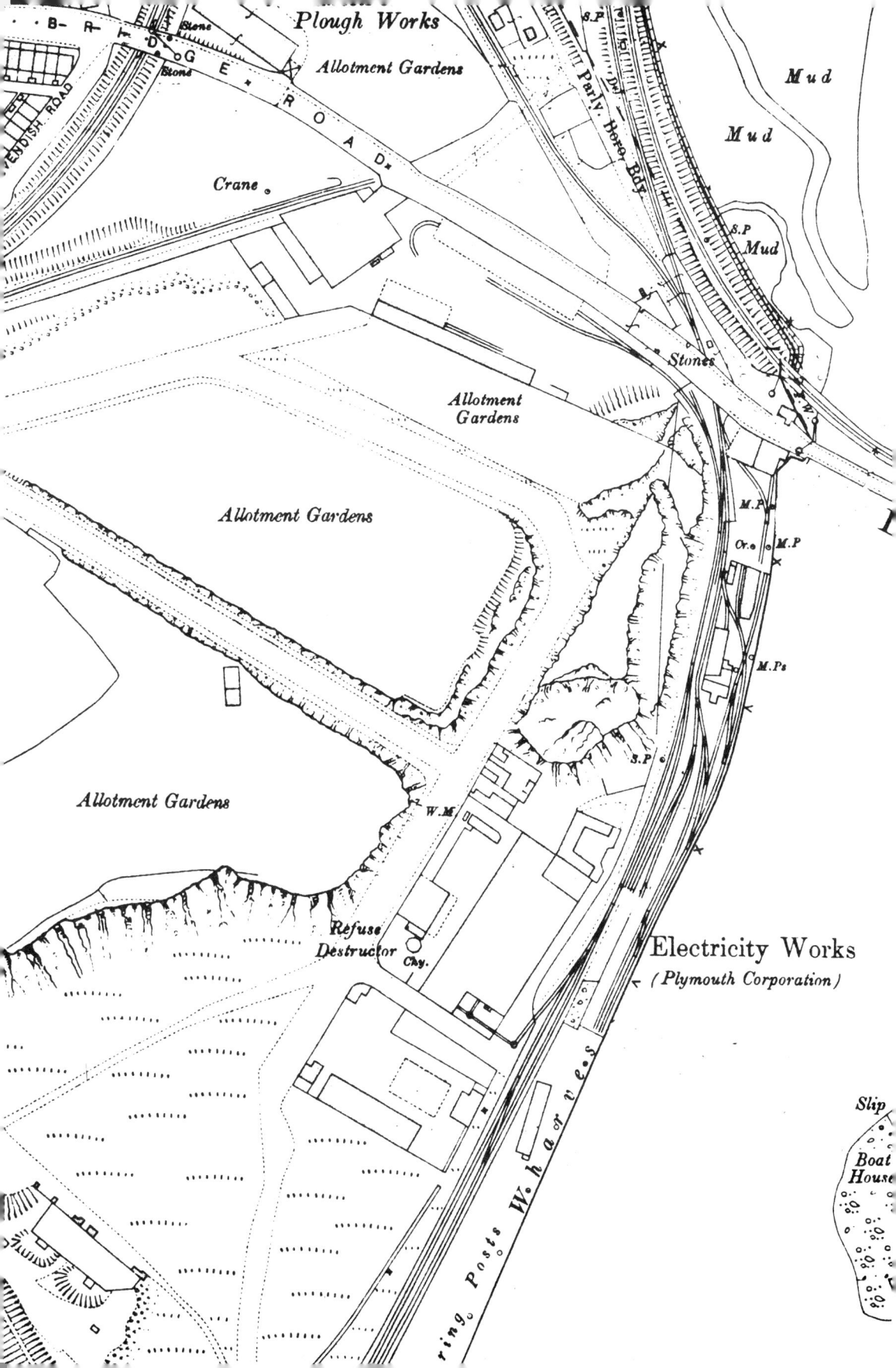

Allotment Gardens

Mud

Mud

Crane

Mud

Stones

Allotment Gardens

Allotment Gardens

Allotment Gardens

Refuse Destructor

Electricity Works
(Plymouth Corporation)

Slip

Boat House

35. Moving further north along the LMT, we look south to see it being cut up in 1962. This part had not been used since 1947. This is Friary Junction, with Lucas Terrace Halt and Friary Shed on the right. The bridge carried the branch trains to Turnchapel. (J.J.Smith)

36. Our journey north now features a 1959 northward view of Mount Gold Junction, the line curving left having been opened on 1st April 1891 by the GWR. It was intended for the use of LSWR trains taking the new route to Friary via Devonport. The crossings on the LMT carried Millbay - Yealmpton passenger services until 1930 but they remained in use until 15th September 1958, after which all freight ran via Friary Yard. Mount Gold and Tothill Halt had been to the right of the photographer from 2nd November 1905 until 1st February 1918. (M.Dart coll.)

37. Still further north, the LMT ran alongside Laira Yard, where there were exchange sidings. Five empty wagons return to Lee Moor, this being the maximum load for two horses. (F.H.Casbourn/M.Dart)

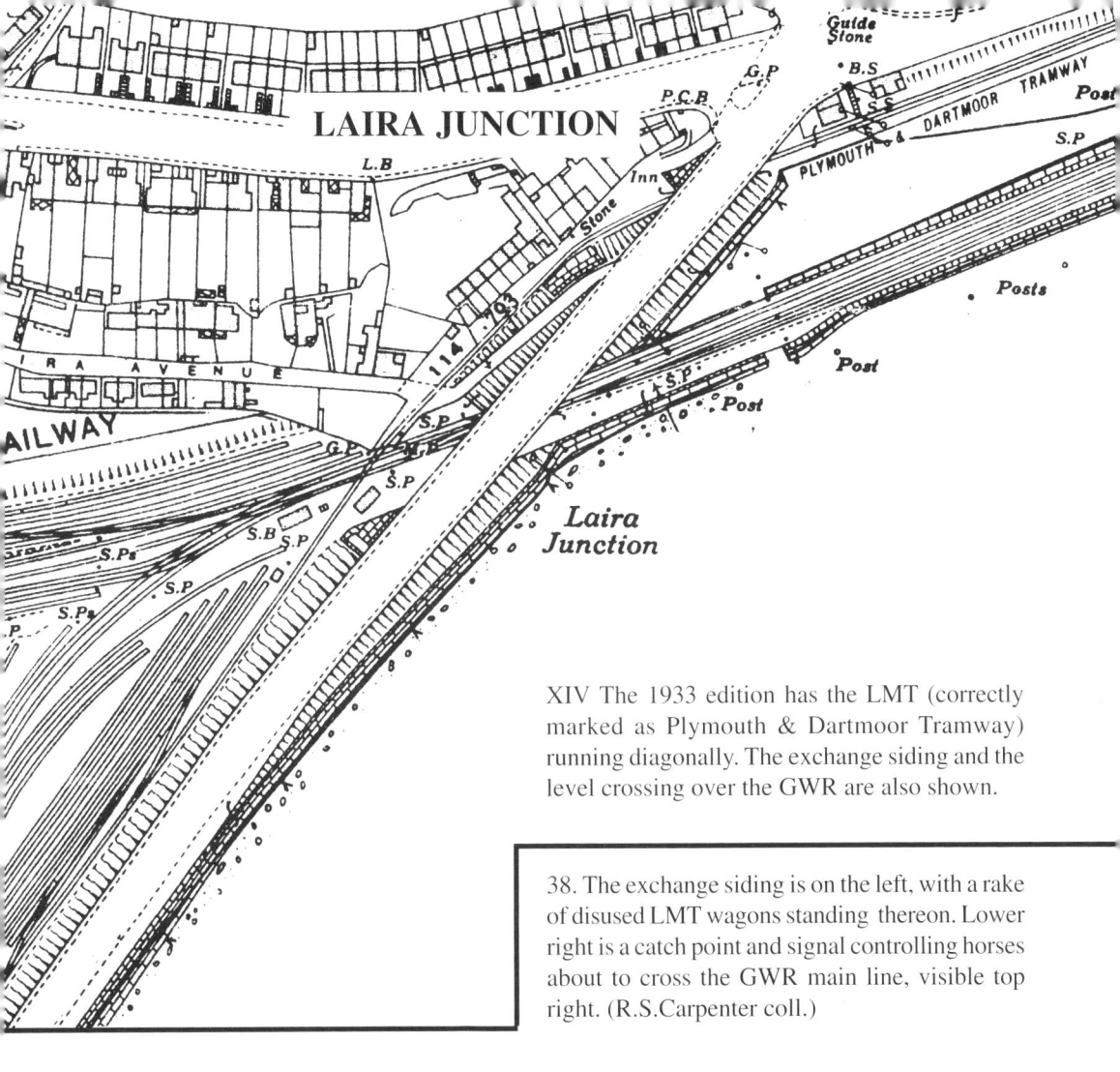

XIV The 1933 edition has the LMT (correctly marked as Plymouth & Dartmoor Tramway) running diagonally. The exchange siding and the level crossing over the GWR are also shown.

38. The exchange siding is on the left, with a rake of disused LMT wagons standing thereon. Lower right is a catch point and signal controlling horses about to cross the GWR main line, visible top right. (R.S.Carpenter coll.)

39. Looking east from the road bridge in April 1949, we can watch the relaying of the skew crossing of the LMT over the main line. The former line was at this site 25 years before the latter was constructed. (F.H.Casbourn/M.Dart)

40. A 1953 view from Laira Junction Box includes the other LMT signal, the remote operated gate lock and the boards required to give the horses a good footing and bridge the point rodding. (R.S.Carpenter coll.)

FRIARY DISTRICT

FRIARY

41. The station opened on 1st July 1891 and had two short and two long passenger platforms throughout its operational life. The centre road often served for engine release.
(Lens of Sutton)

42. Class O2 0-4-4T no. 225 stands in the sun prior to departure for Turnchapel, probably in the 1930s. The compressed air cylinders and additonal hoses were part of the push-pull equipment.
(M.Dart coll.)

43. Yealmpton branch trains used Friary as their city terminus during the 1941-47 service revival. GWR stock was the norm; two autocoaches and 0-6-0PT no. 3705 sufficed on 30th August 1945.
(H.C.Casserley)

XV Friary station is on the left of this 1938 map at 6 ins to 1 mile. It is best examined with reference to map II, which shows the earlier ownerships.

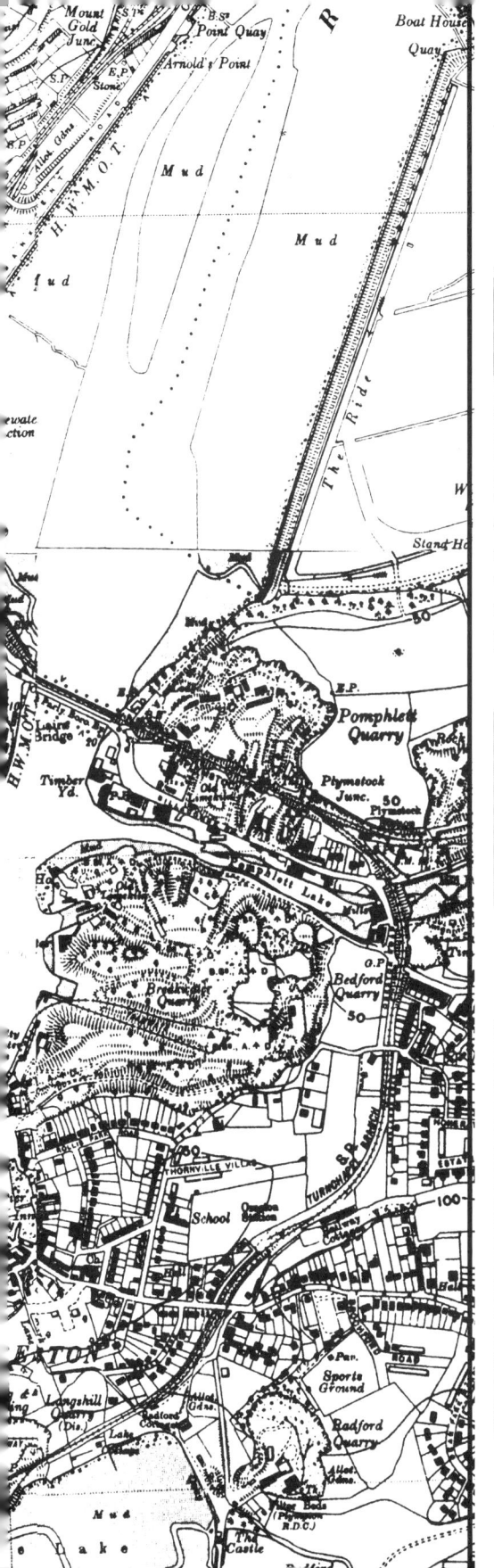

44. A 1957 photograph reveals that the buildings survived the Nazi bombing intact. The entrance was on the north side and two curved approach roads made a gentle descent to it. Demolition took place in 1976. (D.Cullum)

A 25 ins scale map and other photographs of this station can be found in our *Tavistock to Plymouth* album.

PLYMOUTH FRIARY	1928	1936
No. of passenger tickets issued	184546	177714
No. of season tickets issued	297	299
No. of passenger tickets collected	225659	221046
No. of telegrams	14435	16165
No. of parcels forwarded	32004	23224
No. of parcels received	49341	37675
Horses forwarded	52	45
Milk forwarded - Cans 1928/Gallons 1936	344	17
Milk received - Cans 1928/Gallons 1936	7898	20017
General goods forwarded (tons)	117521	124416
General goods received (tons)	62889	48188
Coal, coke etc. received (tons)	17548	2248
Other minerals forwarded (tons)	49223	57261
Other minerals received (tons)	21026	22843
Trucks livestock forwarded	10	4
Trucks livestock received	934	18
Lavatory pennies	2748	5285

45. Another 1957 view includes the main building (right) and "B" Box which functioned until 21st July 1962, although passenger services ceased on 15th September 1958. There had been an engine shed in the far left corner of the site until 1908. (D.Cullum)

46. An RCTS railtour, formed of ex-GWR autocoaches, called on 2nd May 1959. The gong was the "audible means of approach". Many of the sidings and platform roads were used for carriage storage at that time. (F.Hornby)

47. The goods shed that appears in pictures 40 and 44 is beyond the bridge in this view. In the foreground is the single line to Sutton Harbour that descended steeply through a 74 yd long tunnel. (Lens of Sutton)

48. An eastward panorama from the bridge in the previous picture includes "A" Box, which closed on 24th April 1966. Freight traffic was concentrated at this location from 20th June 1966. The picture dates from about 1930 and by 1997 only two little used lines remained. (Lens of Sutton)

49. Ex-LSWR class B4 0-4-0Ts undertook much of the dock shunting on this side of Plymouth. No. 30094 is returning from the Cattewater branch in October 1952 and is passing the approach to Friary loco shed. The main line is not visible, being at a slightly lower level. (M.Dart coll.)

FRIARY SHED

50. The shed came into use in about 1908 and its east end was photographed on 15th June 1926, when L11 class 4-4-0 no. 172 and N class no. A865 were at rest. (H.C.Casserley)

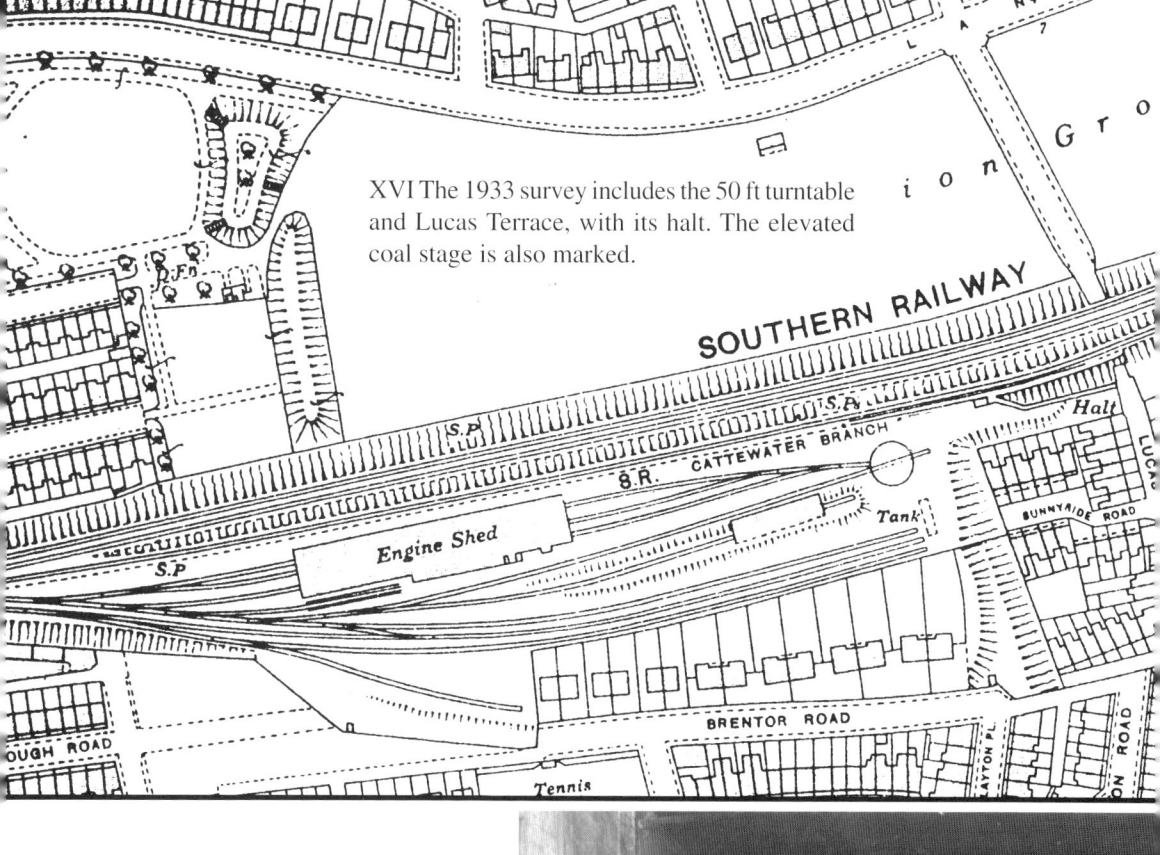

XVI The 1933 survey includes the 50 ft turntable and Lucas Terrace, with its halt. The elevated coal stage is also marked.

51. Class B4 0-4-0T no. 91 stands in the gloomy interior on 30th August 1945. The structure was damaged several times during aerial bombardment. (H.C.Casserley)

52. Ex-GWR Pannier tanks nos 3629 and 4653 were photographed in store near the hoist on 2nd September 1958. The shed closed in May 1963. (L.W.Rowe)

LUCAS TERRACE HALT

53. The windswept halt was in use between October 1905 and 10th September 1951. The platform was extended at the west end in 1923. The bridge seen in picture no. 35 is in the background and the main line from Friary is on the left. (M.Dart coll.)

54. Looking west in September 1963, we see the then recently closed shed and the roofless water tank. The coal stage is beyond the waiting shelter, which, by that time, had been functionless for twelve years. (C.L.Caddy coll.)

55. The 9.03am from Turnchapel was propelled by class O2 no. 30207 on 21st August 1951. The main line is visible between the leading wheels as they approach the halt. (N.W.Sprinks)

CATTEWATER JUNCTION

56. The location of the junction can be established by reference to the right side of map XV. The lines northward from here to Mount Gold Junction were closed on 15th September 1958 and thus do not appear in this photograph taken on 28th June 1962. (J.J.Smith)

57. A southward view from the signal box on the same day includes no. D2177, which has just left the Cattewater branch (right). The box was in use until 1st October 1963. (J.J.Smith)

58. The embankment in the centre of the previous picture was the scene of a derailment of empty cement wagons on 9th March 1978. The diesel from Pomphlet Cement Works was summoned to help resolve the problem. (M.Turvey)

59. A Turnchapel train is seen on Laira Bridge from the LMT tracks on Laira Wharf in the 1930s. The nearer bridge carried the Plymouth-Plymstock road and was rebuilt in concrete. (A.Bray/M.Dart)

60. The spark arrester was a necessary accessory when working on timber wharves. Class B4 no. 30102 was recorded leaving Laira Bridge in August 1957 with timber from Bayly's Yard at Oreston. (D.Richard/M.Dart)

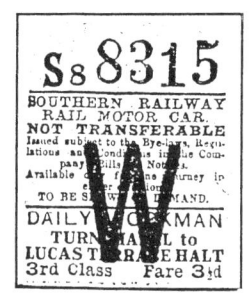

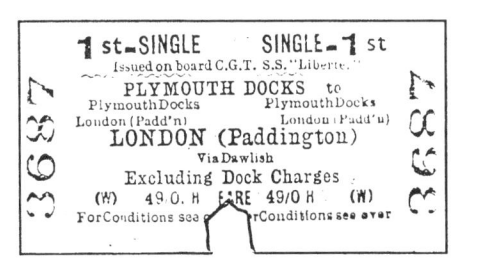

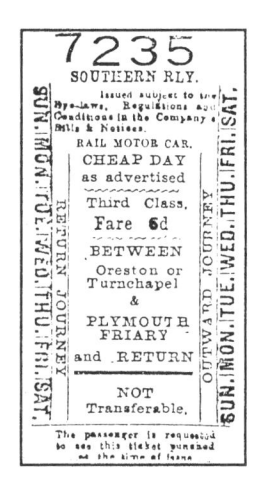

SUTTON HARBOUR BRANCH

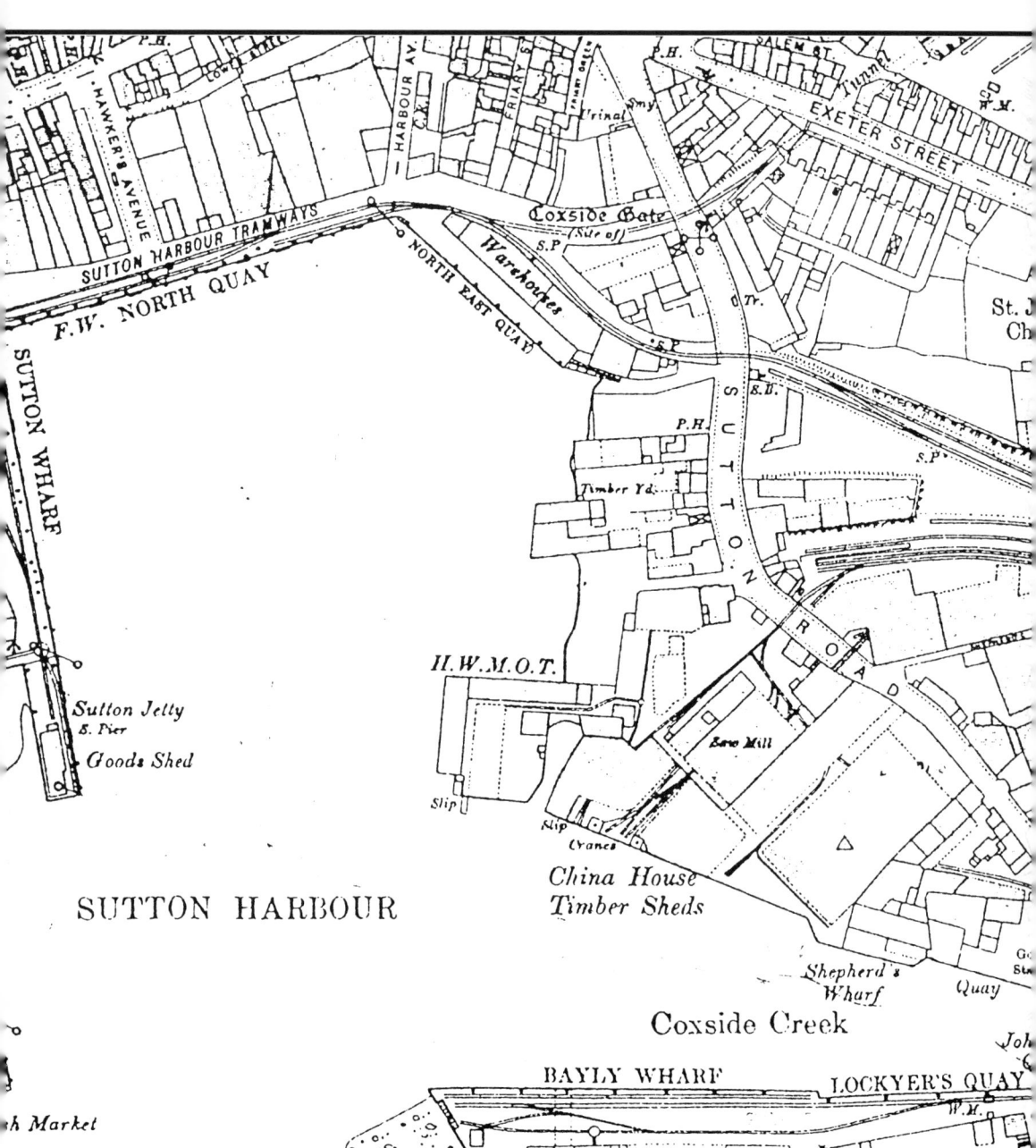

XVII When opened in 1823, the Plymouth & Dartmoor Railway ran both to Laira Wharf and Sutton Pool. The route to the latter was bought by the South Devon Railway and converted to dual 7 ft 0¼ ins and 4 ft 6 ins gauge in 1853. It was entirely horse worked. The lines closed in May 1856 and reopened in October 1857, broad gauge only. Steam traction was introduced in 1869. The branch was bought by the GWR in 1876 and changed to standard gauge in 1892. The North Quay branch came into use on 6th November 1879 and was subject to the same gauge change. Friary Yard and the LSWR connection mentioned in caption 47 are at the top of this 1914 map.

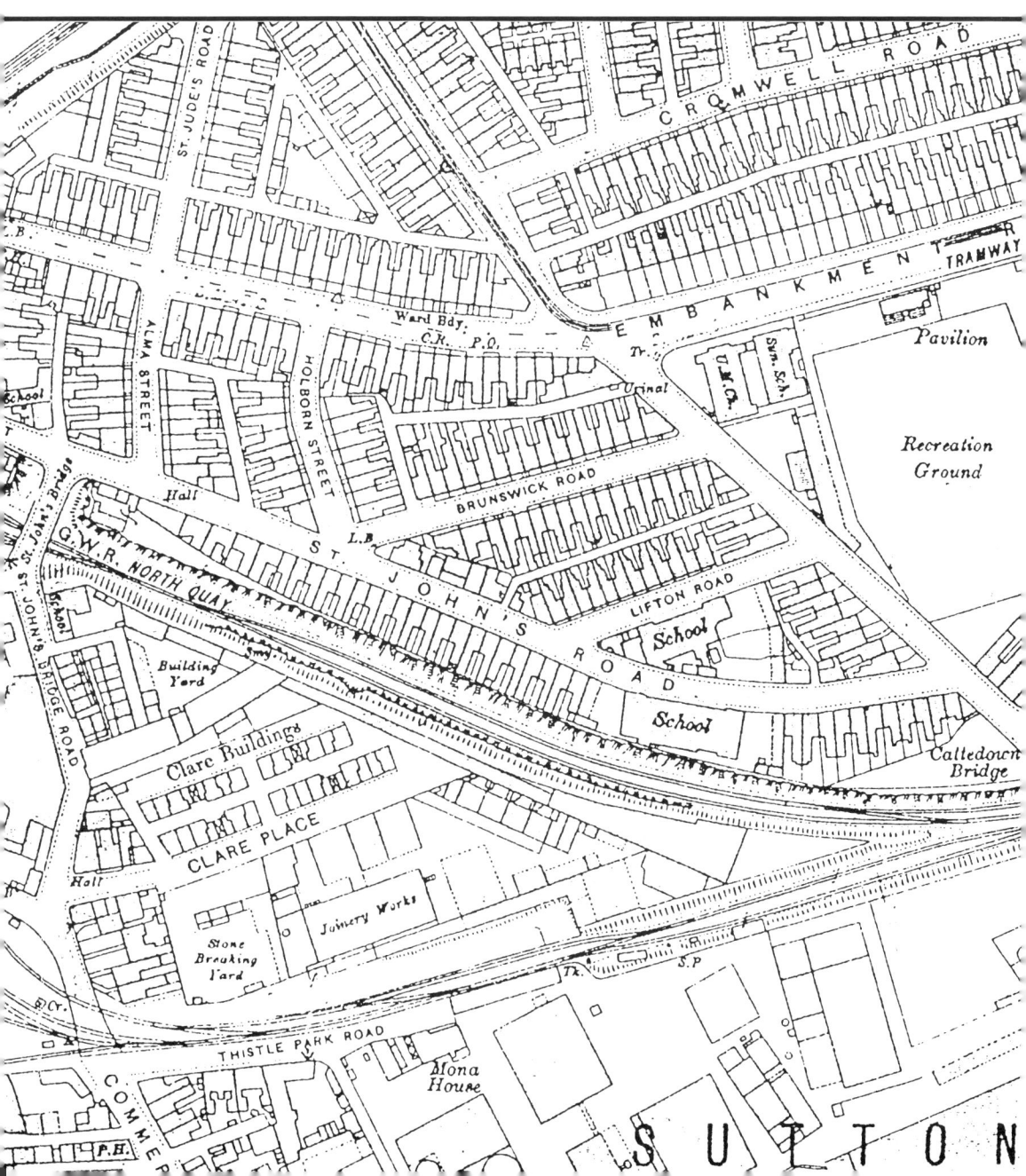

61. Here we look north in 1962, under the Turnchapel branch bridge seen previously in pictures 35 and 53. On the left is the Sutton Harbour branch, which was singled on 23rd November 1936, and on the right is the overgrown LMT which was officially closed in 1961. (J.J.Smith)

62. North Quay Branch Junction is on the right of the previous map (XVII) and is seen from Cattedown Road bridge as class 2021 0-6-0PT no. 2097 leaves the branch. The lines to Sutton Harbour are on the left. (M.Daly)

63. Proceeding towards North Quay, we look west from St. John's Bridge and see Sutton Road Box in the right distance in 1962. The siding on the left was used for several decades by the Plymouth & Stonehouse Gas, Light and Coke Co. Ltd. (J.J.Smith)

64. Sutton Road crossing was at the west end of a long loop which started at St. John's Bridge, visible in the background. The gates were padlocked and hand operated. (J.J.Smith)

65. The LSWR line from Friary emerged from its tunnel and promptly crossed Sutton Road on this level crossing. There had been a signal box here until November 1950; the line closed at that time and was lifted in 1957. (J.J.Smith)

66. Evidence of the presence of the LSWR was still to be seen on the north elevation of a building on South Wharf in 1996. All traffic to Sutton Harbour had ceased by 1969. (V.Mitchell)

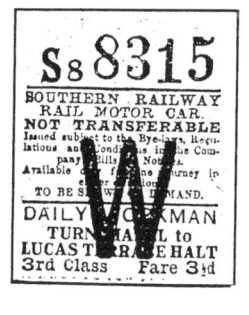

67. Commercial Road crossing on the original route to Sutton Harbour was photographed in 1962. Looking north we have the line to Lockyer's Quay and Bayly's Wharf passing under the first gate on the left, the others leading to the goods depot. The gates on the right were still in use in 1997 on a motor dealer's premises. (J.J.Smith)

68. Activity at Bayly's Wharf was recorded on a postcard. The private sidings were developed around the turn of the century and were available for use until December 1973. (M.Dart coll.)

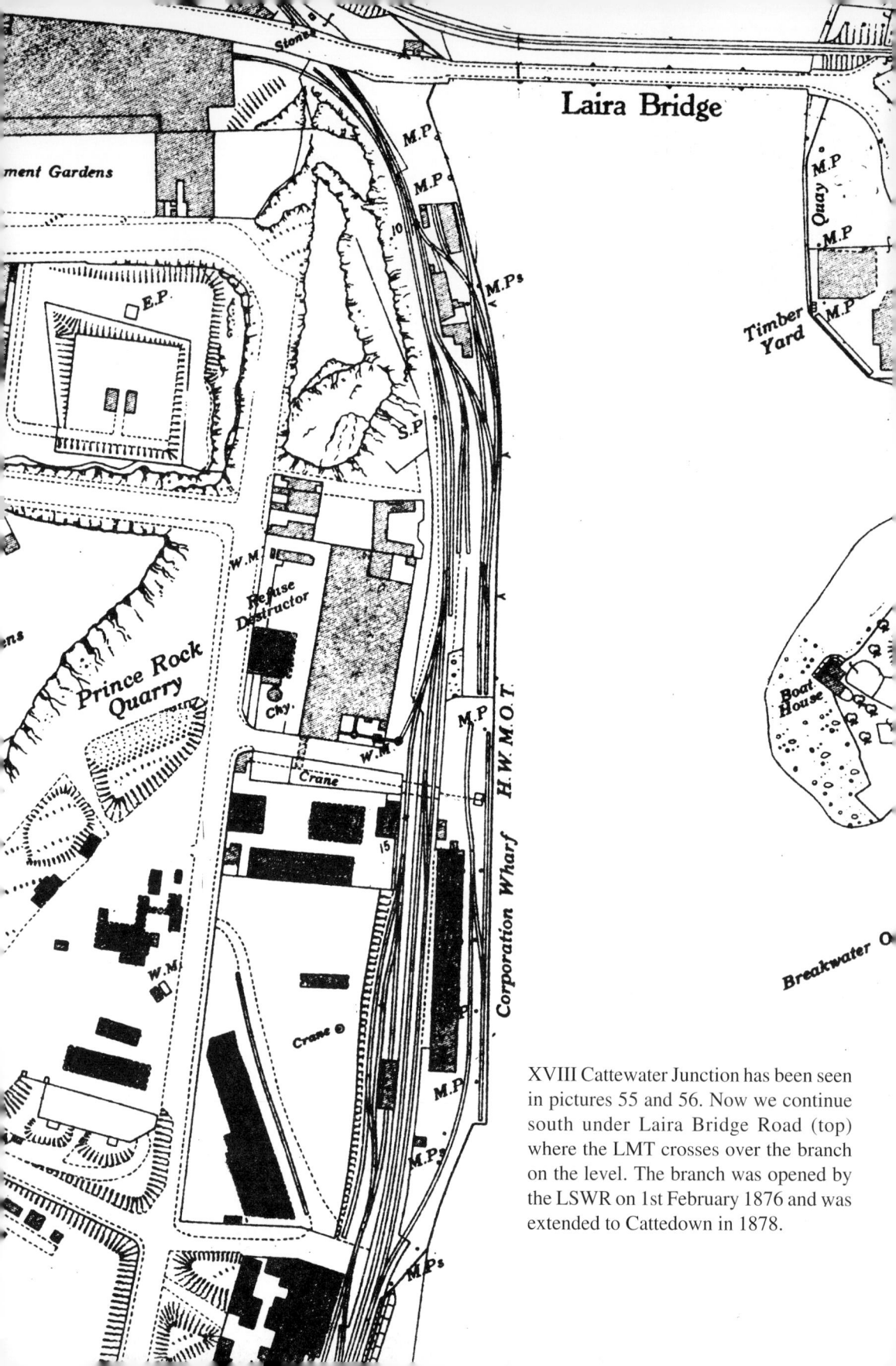

XVIII Cattewater Junction has been seen in pictures 55 and 56. Now we continue south under Laira Bridge Road (top) where the LMT crosses over the branch on the level. The branch was opened by the LSWR on 1st February 1876 and was extended to Cattedown in 1878.

CATTEWATER BRANCH

69. A northward view under the widened road bridge in 1962 shows the disused LMT crossing the branch to reach Laira Wharf, which is behind the photographer. The points once served a siding which curved sharply left to Rethick's Yard and stone workshops. (J.J.Smith)

70. Class B4 no. 88 was recorded shunting south of Laira Wharf on 19th June 1950, 2½ years after it has ceased to be "Southern" property. Turnchapel can be seen across Cattewater Harbour. (J.J.Smith)

71. An eastward panorama from above Cattewater Tunnel in June 1962 includes the BP Depot, the siding (left foreground) for which was in use from 1922 to 1969. The siding on the left was used by Regent Oil from 1952 until 1966. A new level crossing occupied the site in 1997. (J.J.Smith)

XIX The 1914 map includes Cattewater Goods, west of the tunnel. The area east thereof was developed as shown in picture no. 71.

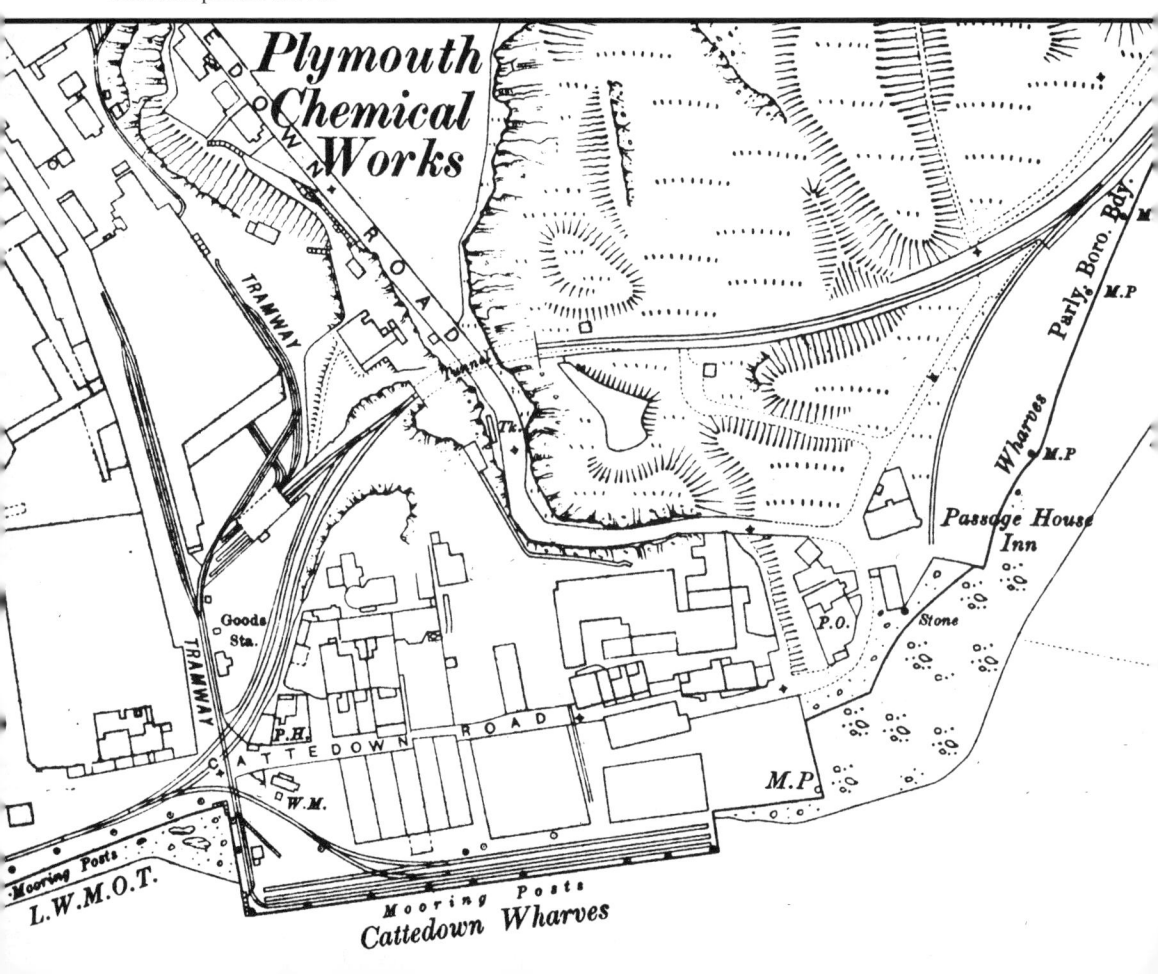

72. The west portal of the 74 yd-long Cattewater Tunnel was recorded in 1970. The goods sidings on the left were originally LSWR property, whereas most sidings off the branch were private. (M.Dart)

73. The same points were photographed from above the tunnel in May 1952 as a B4 tank passes the former LSWR goods shed. (M.Daly)

74. Three empty bitumen tanks were in tow as no. 08819 leaves the Conoco terminal on 7th November 1995. (D.Mitchell)

75. A view south from Cattedown Road in July 1993 shows the extent of the Esso Bitumen Plant. A shield was required to protect workers and stock from loose limestone. (T.Corin)

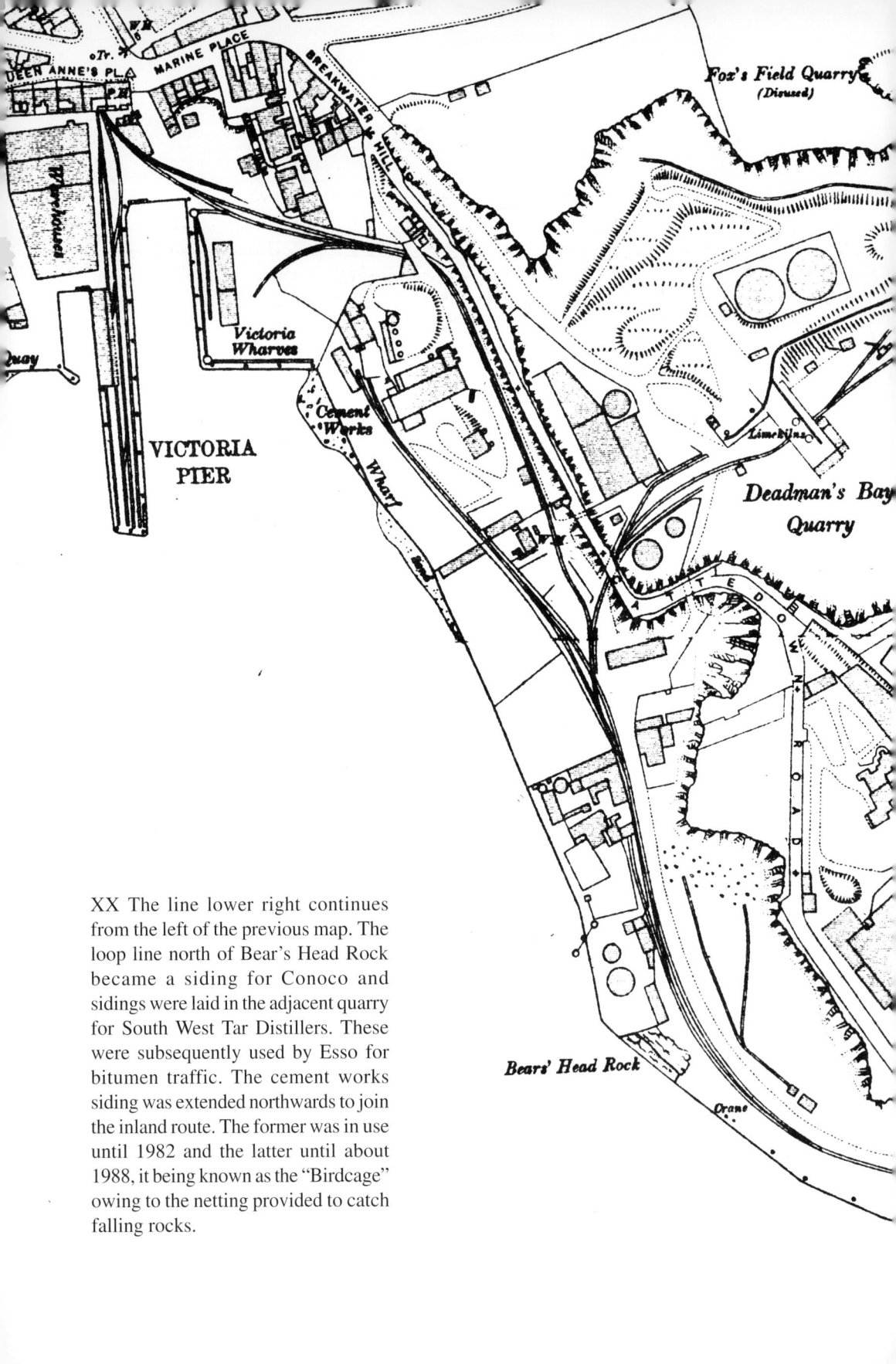

XX The line lower right continues from the left of the previous map. The loop line north of Bear's Head Rock became a siding for Conoco and sidings were laid in the adjacent quarry for South West Tar Distillers. These were subsequently used by Esso for bitumen traffic. The cement works siding was extended northwards to join the inland route. The former was in use until 1982 and the latter until about 1988, it being known as the "Birdcage" owing to the netting provided to catch falling rocks.

76. A glimpse through the gates on 28th April 1997 shows an 0-4-0 and an 0-6-0 Sentinel diesel in attendance. The siding on the left was added in 1982. (V.Mitchell)

77. A northward view at about the centre of map XX in 1971 shows the "Birdcage" route along the foot of the cliffs. Curving sharply right from it is a line that passes through a short tunnel to an Esso Depot. (M.Dart)

78. The Anglo-American Oil Company made a private siding agreement in 1898 in connection with its oil store built in Deadman's Bay Quarry. It later became Esso property and class 03 no. D2134 was photographed leaving the site on 25th October 1971. (M.Dart)

79. We are now nearing the top of map XX and looking at the limit of BR property on 17th May 1952. Included in the view is Victoria Pier (right), Harvey's coal yard and part of South West Tar Distilleries premises. (M.Daly)

VICTORIA WHARF

80. Victoria Wharf always provided their own motive power. *Alicie* is a Leeds-built Manning Wardle which was reputed to have been converted to an 0-6-0ST. (Victoria Wharf)

CATTEWATER BRANCH.

This branch, which is connected with the Turnchapel Branch at Cattewater Junction, is worked as an ordinary shunting yard. One or more engines may be permitted on the branch at one time, as ordered by the Station Master at Plymouth Friary, who will provide a competent Shunter to take charge of, and remain with, each engine during the time it is engaged on the branch.

Shunters must be careful to see that engines are moved cautiously, and at a low speed, from one part of the Cattewater line to another ; must satisfy themselves, before allowing the trains to be moved, that the lines are clear for their passage, and must at all times keep a careful look-out for other trains, and shunting operations, and see that the several level crossings on the branch are clear.

The load of a train from Plymouth Friary to Cattewater must not exceed 60 wagons and one brake van ; and from Cattewater to Plymouth Friary the load must not exceed equal to 30 loaded goods wagons and one brake van.

The passage of trains between Cattewater Junction and Prince Rock level crossing is controlled by means of bell signals between those points.

The gates fencing the China Clay Company's tram line, which crosses the branch line on the level at a point adjacent to Prince Rock level crossing, must be placed across the tram line and the gates of the Prince Rock level crossing must be placed across the roadway; the respective gates must be secured in that position by padlocks before permission is given for a train to enter or leave the Cattewater Branch.

81. The turntable shown on map XX was replaced at an unrecorded date by two complex dual gauge points. The corner of the dock had to be spanned.
(Victoria Wharf)

82. The span in the previous picture is also included in this one which features bagged china clay being loaded into a ship. This dry material had to be conveyed in vans, as seen in the background.
(ECC coll.)

83. There was more dual gauge track on Victoria Pier but there was a standard gauge crane as well. All rail movements to and from the pier necessitated reversal in a short tunnel. (Victoria Wharf)

84. Close examination of map XX will reveal that the headshunt was in a single ended tunnel, adjacent to the cellar of a public house. It doubled up as an engine shed - Planet no. 3281 was therein on 7th June 1970. (M.Dart)

TURNCHAPEL BRANCH
PLYMSTOCK

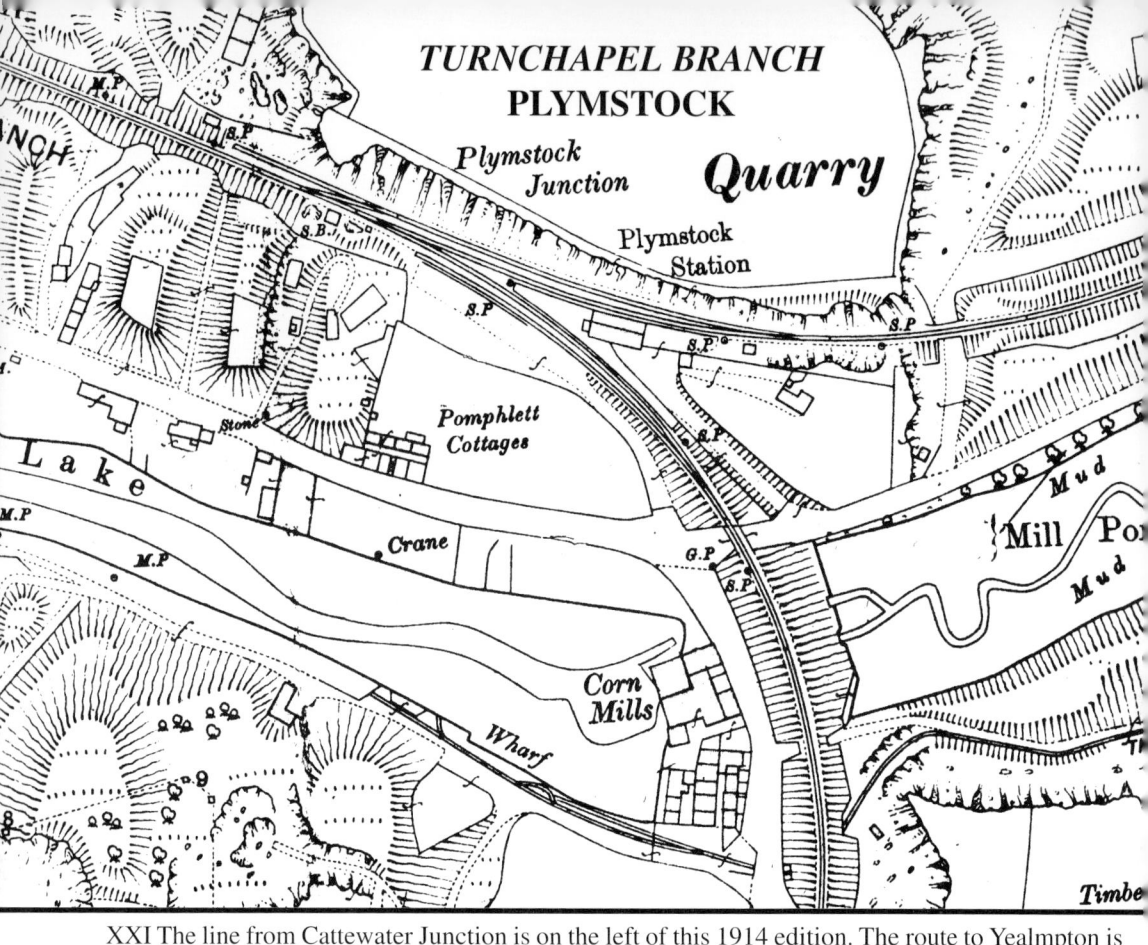

XXI The line from Cattewater Junction is on the left of this 1914 edition. The route to Yealmpton is on the right and we take the Turnchapel line which runs south. The former GWR side of the station is shown in pictures 100 to 106 in this volume.

85. We can now enjoy two photographs from 2nd May 1959. A train from Turnchapel approaches from the south while another special waits in the Yealmpton branch platform. The road to the goods yard is also evident. (R.M.Casserley)

86. Having drawn alongside the goods loop, we can see that the train is a special for the RCTS composed of "Plymouth Gate" stock propelled by class O2 no. 30182. The loading dock is beyond the mound of coal. (R.M.Casserley)

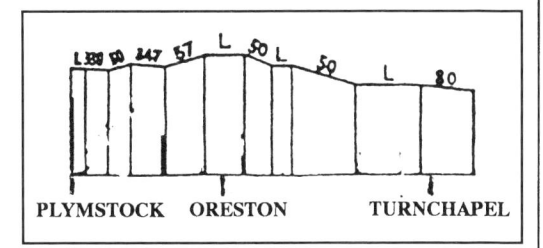

PLYMSTOCK	1928	1936
No. of passenger tickets issued	29589	21837
No. of season tickets issued	302	64
No. of passenger tickets collected	55950	30298
No. of telegrams	-	-
No. of parcels forwarded	193	138
No. of parcels received	937	3542
Horses forwarded	1	1
Milk forwarded - Cans 1928/Gallons 1936	-	-
Milk received - Cans 1928/Gallons 1936	-	-
General goods forwarded (tons)	1013	1829
General goods received (tons)	1050	2391
Coal, coke etc. received (tons)	1422	1619
Other minerals forwarded (tons)	17	27
Other minerals received (tons)	209	262
Trucks livestock forwarded	1	-
Trucks livestock received	1	2
Lavatory pennies	168	72

ORESTON

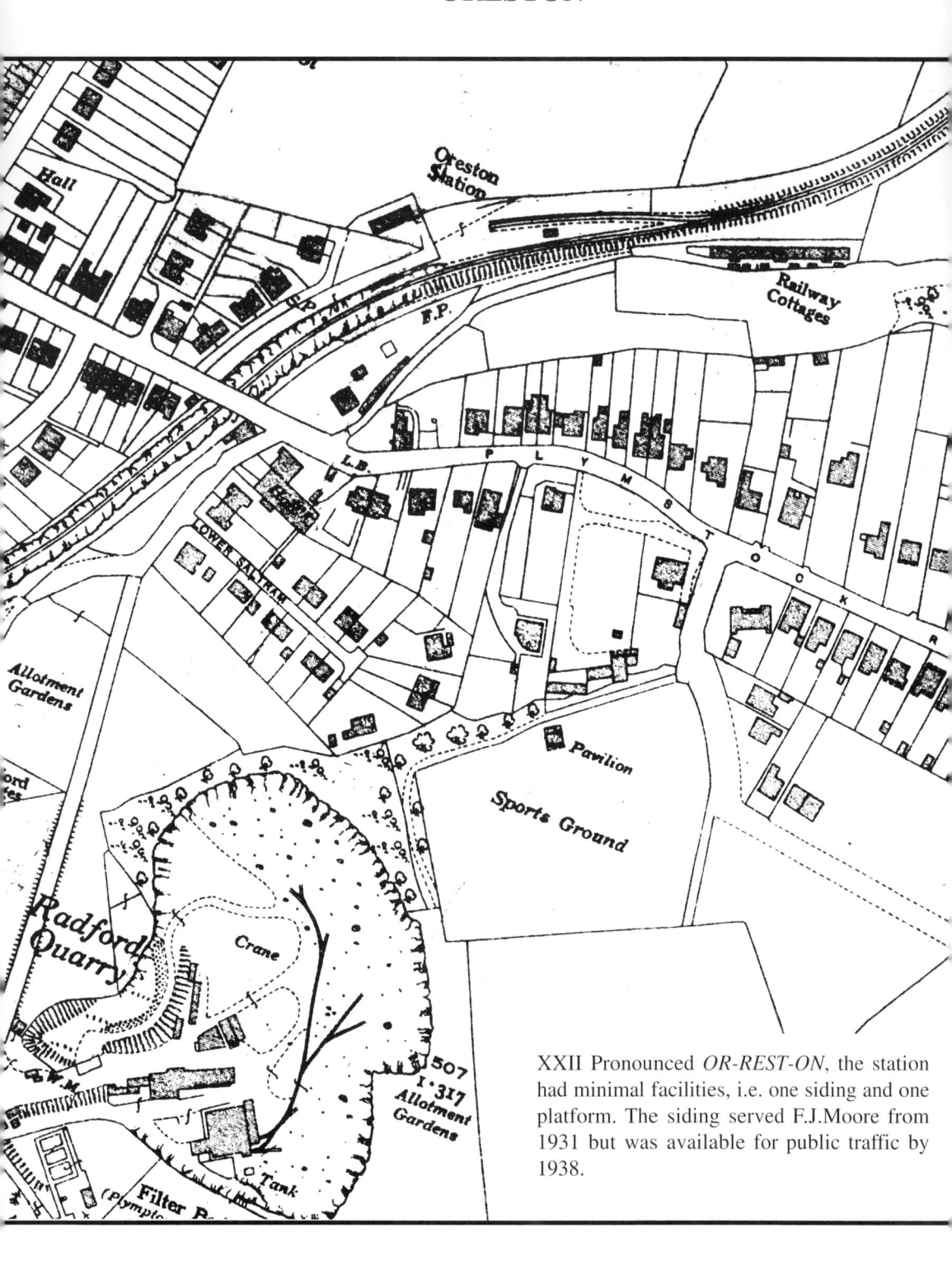

XXII Pronounced *OR-REST-ON*, the station had minimal facilities, i.e. one siding and one platform. The siding served F.J.Moore from 1931 but was available for public traffic by 1938.

87. Class O2 no. 30182 waits with the 1.3pm from Turnchapel on 19th June 1950. A loaded coal wagon and a battered mechanical horse stand in the goods yard. (J.J.Smith)

88. The goods dock is evident in this picture taken after freight facilities had been withdrawn on 1st October 1961. There is now no trace of railway occupation of the site. (M.Dart coll.)

WEST OF ORESTON

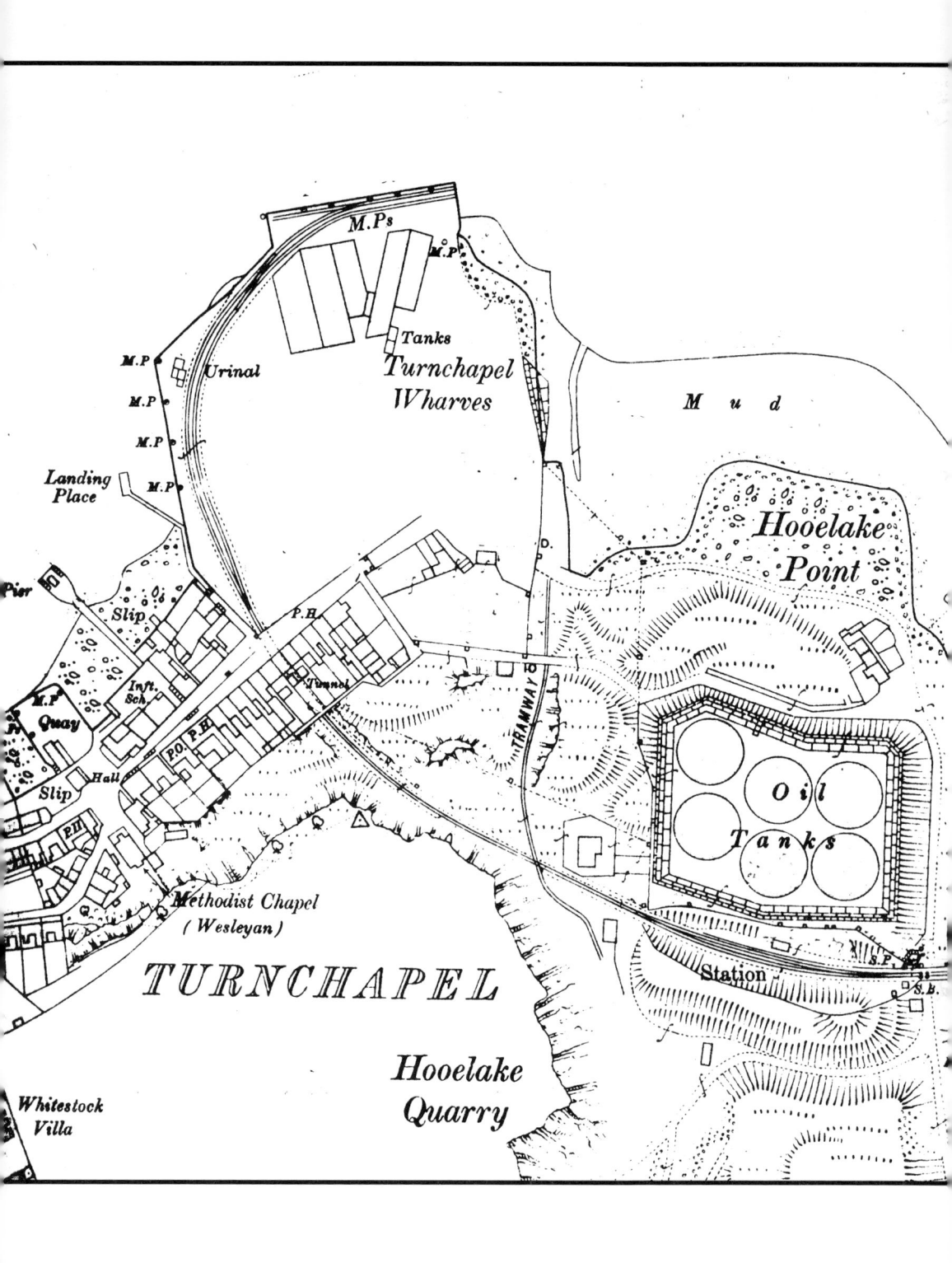

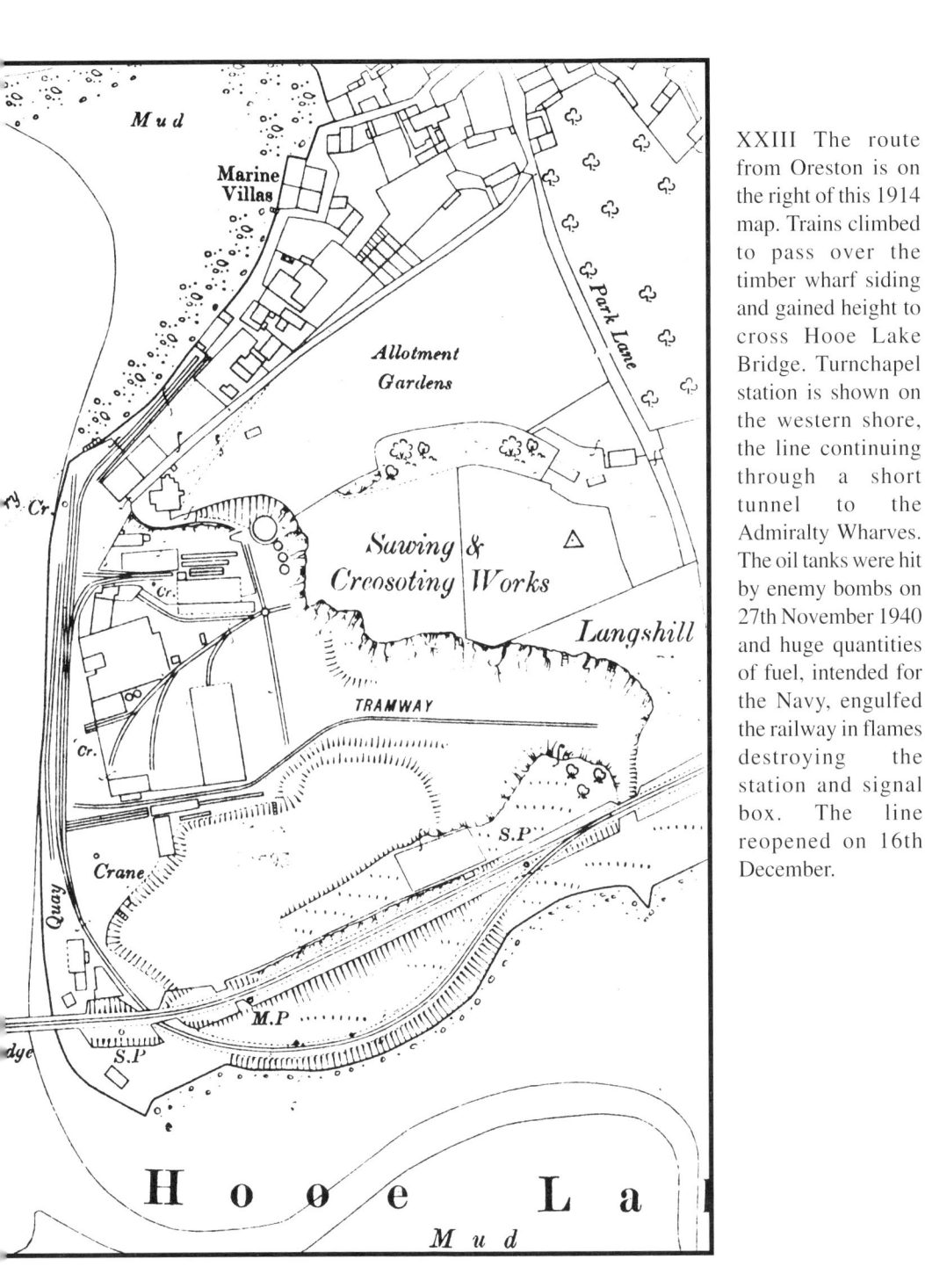

XXIII The route from Oreston is on the right of this 1914 map. Trains climbed to pass over the timber wharf siding and gained height to cross Hooe Lake Bridge. Turnchapel station is shown on the western shore, the line continuing through a short tunnel to the Admiralty Wharves. The oil tanks were hit by enemy bombs on 27th November 1940 and huge quantities of fuel, intended for the Navy, engulfed the railway in flames destroying the station and signal box. The line reopened on 16th December.

89. Bayly's Wharf was occupied by the Plymouth & Oreston Timber Company for many decades. Creosoted poles, sleepers and timber was the main output but rail traffic ceased on 17th October 1961. This is the view from a passing train two weeks earlier. (M.Dart)

90. The swing bridge over Hooe Lake was hand cranked by the signalman, who was isolated on the span while it was open. A figure stands near the mast as a ship waits for a LSWR train to pass. A few stacks of timber stand on the right. (Lens of Sutton)

91. A splendid photograph from 14th June 1926 shows the lone fireman on class O2 0-4-4T no. E233, the lattice gates which gave the coaches their name, a solitary passenger, the guard and the driver. A fine profile of branch travel. (H.C.Casserley)

TURNCHAPEL

92. The signalman receives the single line tablet outside the small station building in the LSWR era. No. 80 was an 0-4-4T of class T1 and was in use from 1890 until 1936. (Lens of Sutton)

93. The entrance to the station was recorded on 8th July 1924, as class O2 no. 218 propels its train onto the bridge. A rear lamp and a headcode disc were permitted simultaneously. (H.C.Casserley)

94. Class O2 no. s182 approaches the signalman on 23rd June 1949. The original signal box base can be seen at the end of the bridge. The compressor in the wagon suggests bridge maintenance in progress. (S.C.Nash)

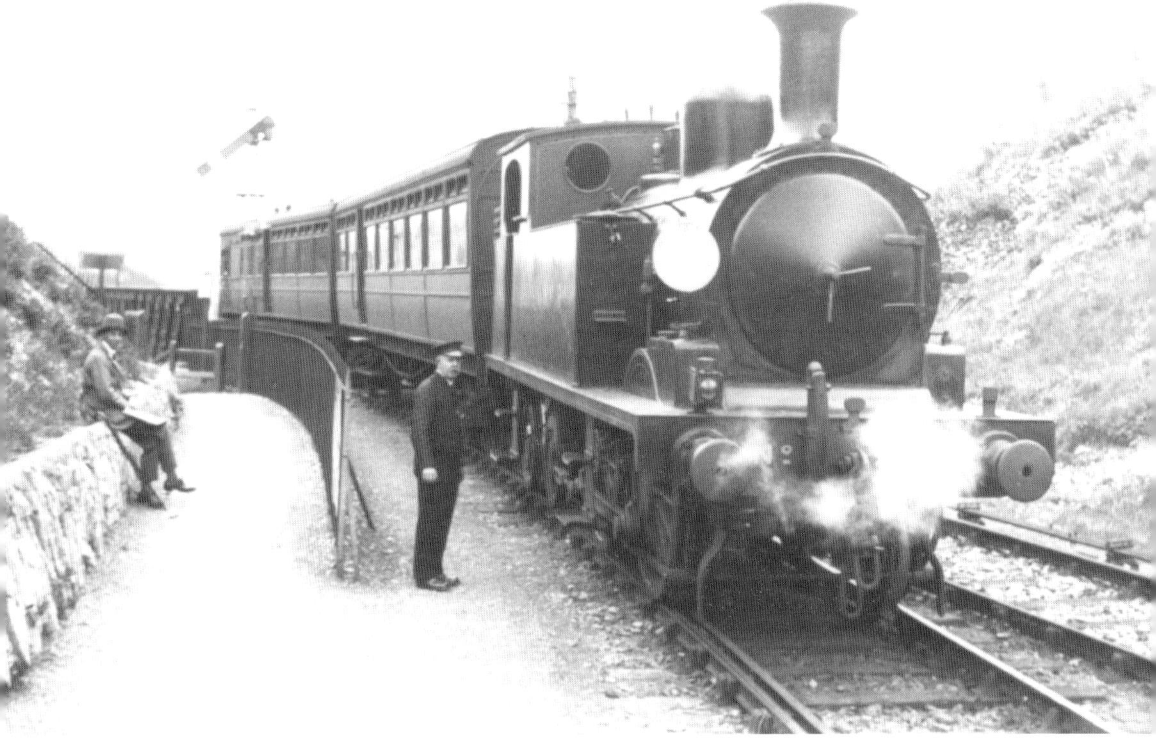

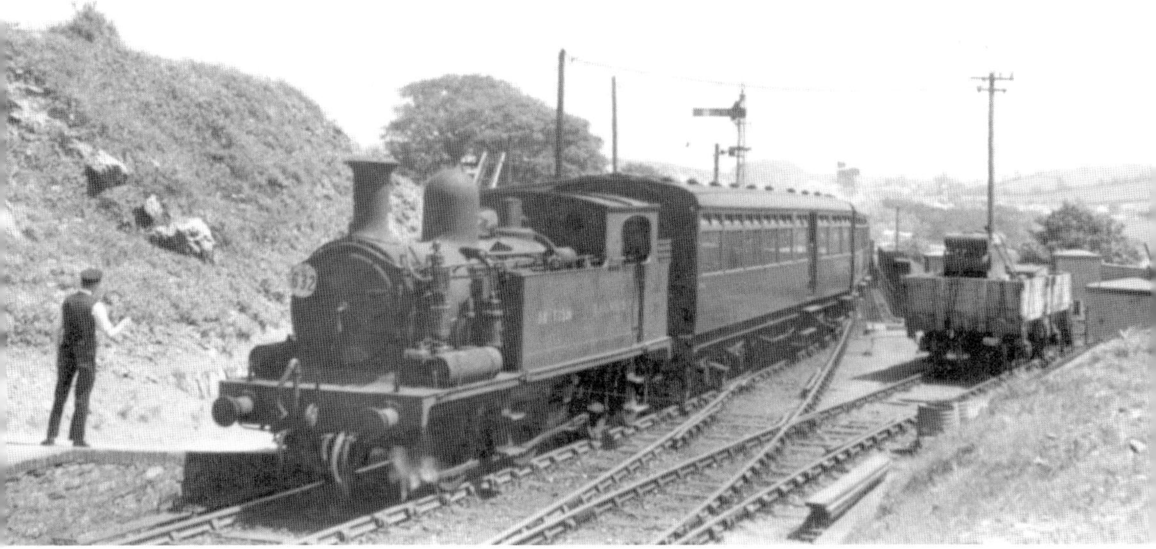

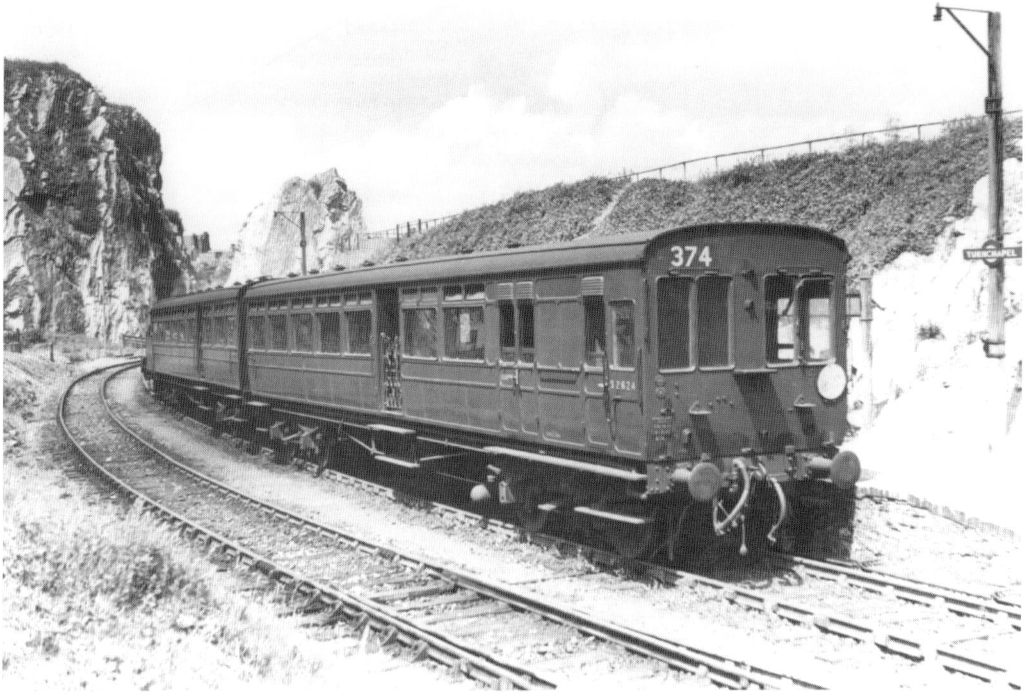
374

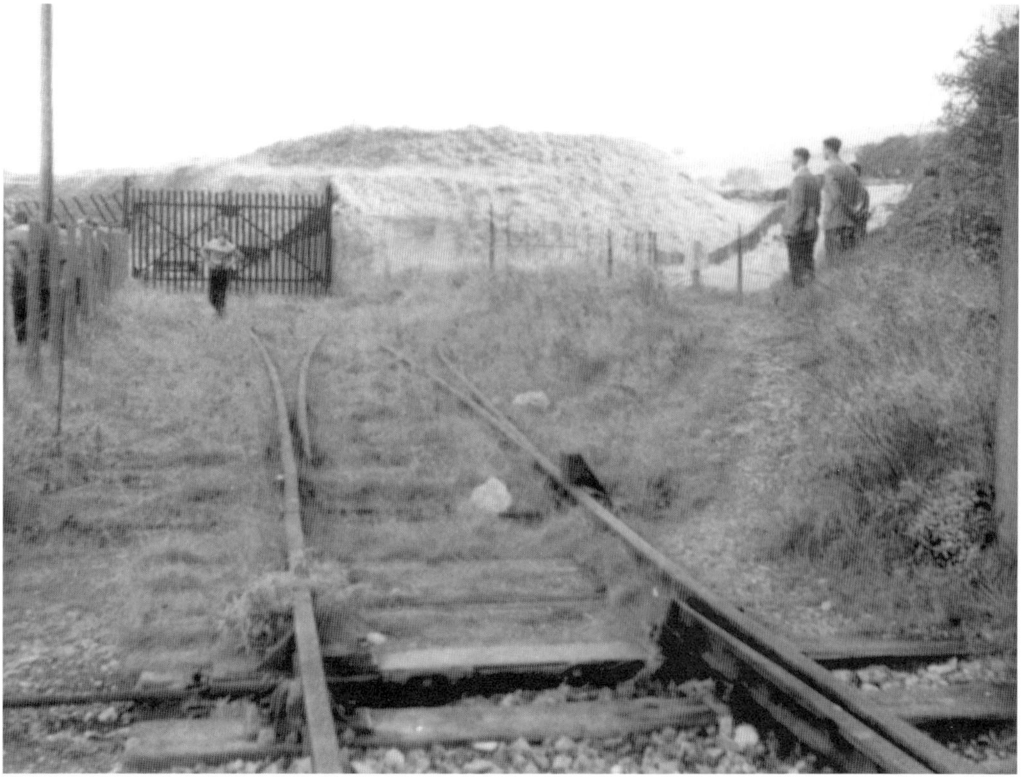

95. A 1950 photograph includes the gate (left) on a siding which served Moore's Quarry from 1927 and the Air Ministry from 1944. The boundary fence for the oil tank site is included. (J.J.Smith)

TURNCHAPEL	1928	1936
No. of passenger tickets issued	39224	42180
No. of season tickets issued	162	69
No. of passenger tickets collected	54498	95610
No. of telegrams	-	-
No. of parcels forwarded	51	79
No. of parcels received	293	1220
Horses forwarded	-	-
Milk forwarded - Cans 1928/Gallons 1936	-	-
Milk received - Cans 1928/Gallons 1936	-	-
General goods forwarded (tons)	5	13
General goods received (tons)	10	62
Coal, coke etc. received (tons)	-	-
Other minerals forwarded (tons)	261	-
Other minerals received (tons)	-	-
Trucks livestock forwarded	-	-
Trucks livestock received	-	-
Lavatory pennies	-	-

96. The siding west of the station branched to enter an Air Ministry fuel store and an ordnance depot. This photograph was taken on 30th September 1961, as were the two that follow. (M.Dart)

97. The special train that day was hired by the Plymouth Railway Circle and hauled by class M7 no. 30034. The signal box had opened on 8th March 1942 and was closed on 30th October 1961, when all traffic ceased. (M.Dart)

98. A westward view from the end of the station area includes the tunnel marked on the map. The siding on Turnchapel Wharf was originally provided for Messrs. Bulteel. (M.Dart)

99. The line emerged from the tunnel onto Admiralty property, where a loop and several sidings had once been in use. Security had prevented any photography when they were in traffic. (M.Daly)

YEALMPTON BRANCH
PLYMSTOCK

100. Having seen the south side of the station in pictures 85 and 86, we can now look at the Yealmpton platform and its loop line (left). Although an LSWR station, no canopy was provided for its passengers. (Lens of Sutton)

101. Class B4 0-4-0T no. 30083 has shunted back into the Yealmpton branch, having worked a return trip to Bayly's Wharf. The signal on the left was termed "Up Main"; the other was "Up Branch". The date is 20th June 1950. (J.J.Smith)

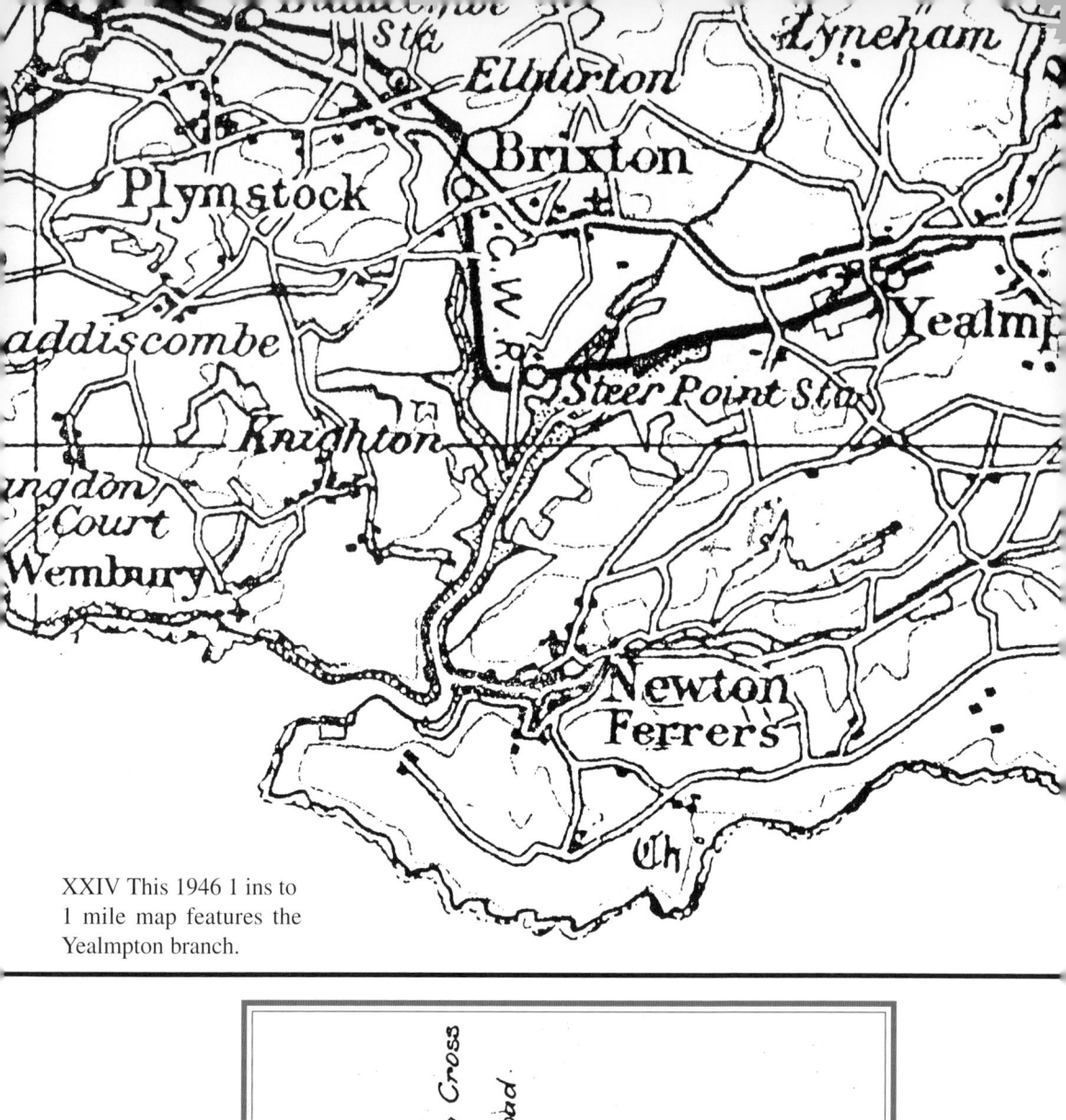

XXIV This 1946 1 ins to 1 mile map features the Yealmpton branch.

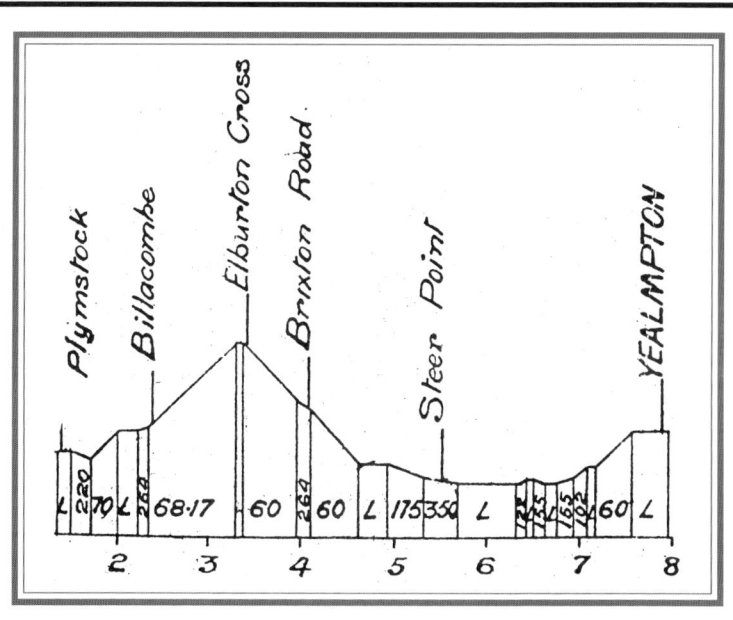

102. Seen on the same day is no. 30182 propelling the 1.3pm from Turnchapel, while 0-6-0PT no. 4693 is working a freight service from Yealmpton and a local coalman is at work in a wagon. (J.J.Smith)

103. A closer look at the train in the background reveals a decrepit coach. It had been stored on the branch and was making its final journey to the scrapyard. The loading dock and catch points on the up siding are also visible. (J.J.Smith)

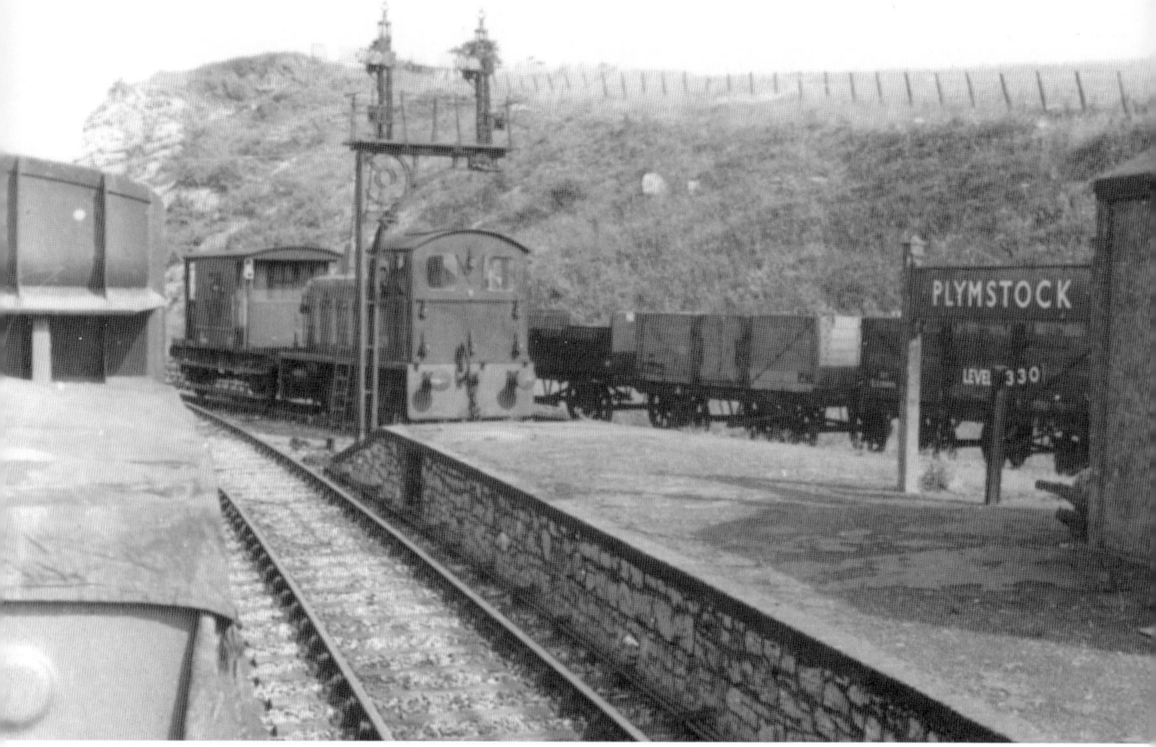
PLYMSTOCK

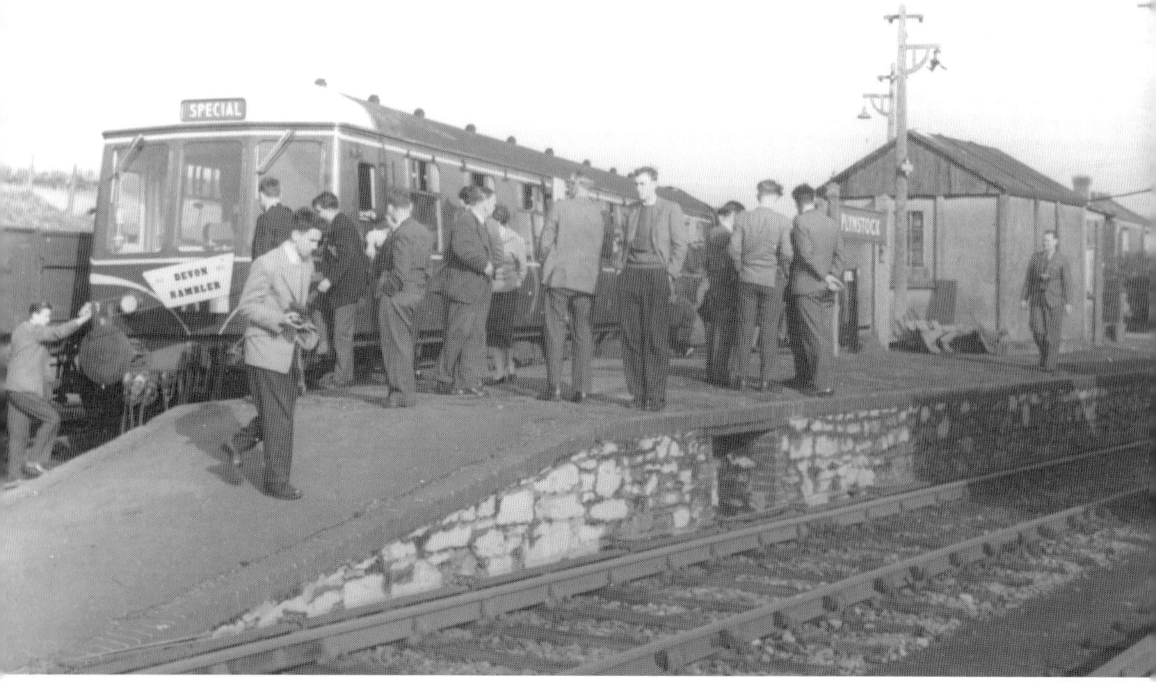
SPECIAL
DEVON RAMBLER
PLYMSTOCK

104. General freight traffic continued until 7th October 1963 and was diesel worked towards the end. The signal box shown on map XXI was closed on 14th July 1935, when a frame was provided in the booking office. (Lens of Sutton)

105. The station buildings were destroyed during an air raid in 1941 and were replaced by prefabricated structures, largely made of concrete. The goods shed is seen on 11th April 1959, along with the Railway Enthusiasts Club special seen several times on the following pages.
(A.E.Bennett)

106. The 1941 signal box had a ticket office at the rear. A new siding (left) was laid in June 1963 to serve the Associated Portland Cement Company's new works, and was photographed in December. The station site was cleared later and four parallel lines laid, plus two sidings for the unloading of butane for the South West Gas Board. Cement traffic ceased in February 1987 but the gas traffic diminished and ended earlier. All track was lifted in 1994 and there is now no trace of railway activity in the area.
(C.L.Caddy coll.)

BILLACOMBE

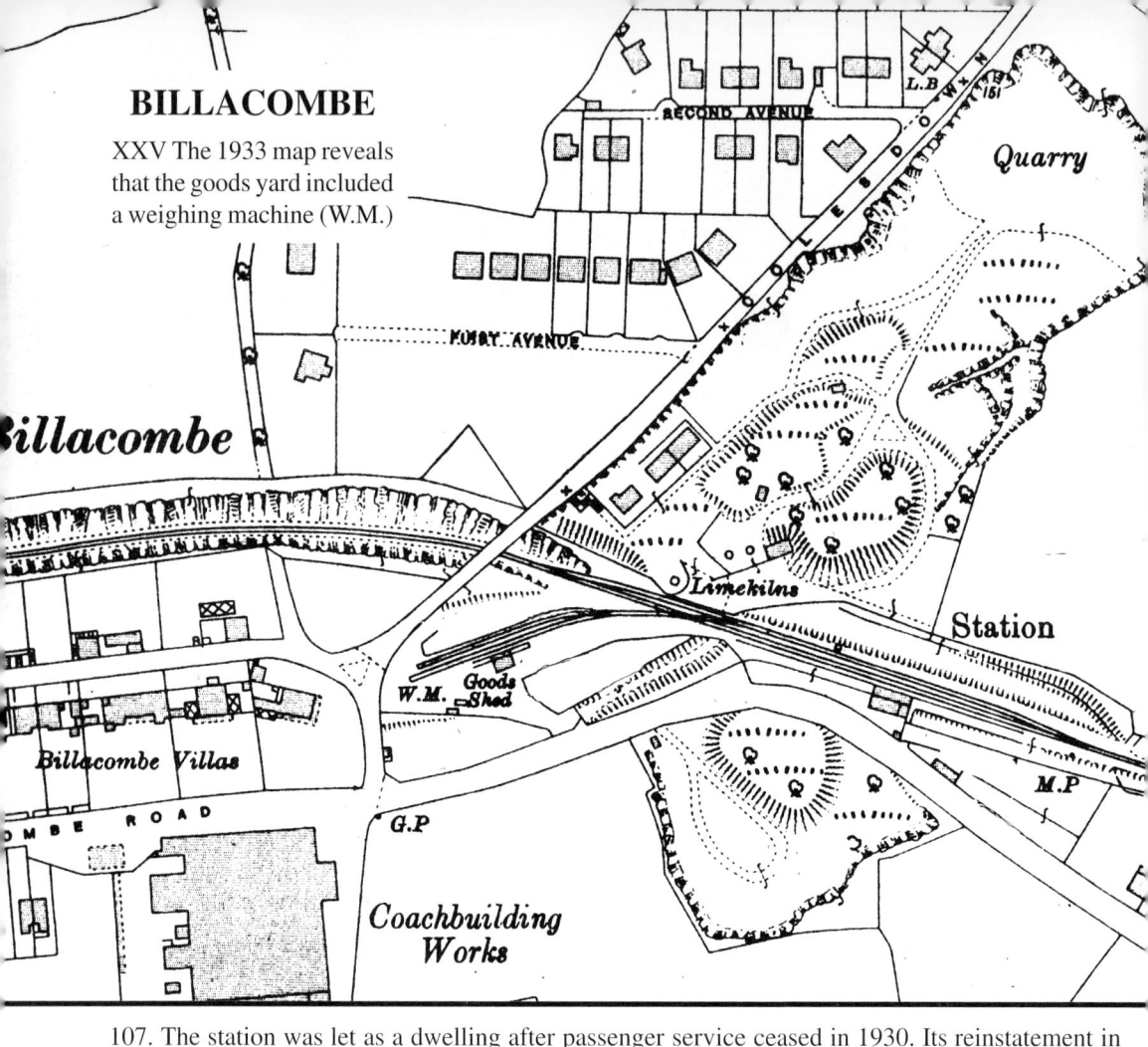

XXV The 1933 map reveals that the goods yard included a weighing machine (W.M.)

107. The station was let as a dwelling after passenger service ceased in 1930. Its reinstatement in 1941 necessitated segregation of travellers from residents by means of a fence. Ex-GWR 0-6-0PT no. 4693 is shunting the yard on 20th June 1950. The ground frame is silhouetted against a lime kiln. (J.J.Smith)

108. The train mentioned in caption 105 was recorded on its way to Yealmpton; it was the only DMU to traverse the branch. The building was later dismantled for re-erection at Marsh Mills on the Plym Valley Railway, having been used for a short period as an ECC laboratory for analysis of quarry products.
(A.E.Bennett)

BILLACOMBE	1903	1913	1923	1933
Passenger tickets issued	5901	7412	3613	
Season tickets issued	*	*	33	
Parcels forwarded	499	861	332	
General goods forwarded (tons)	127	119	76	149
Coal and coke received (tons)	128	202	1915	225
Other minerals received (tons)	930	651	2223	329
General goods received (tons)	60	296	328.	208
Trucks of livestock handled	-	-	-	-

(* not available)

109. A 1960 photograph reveals the reason why the locomotive is in the loop in picture 107. Over 3000 tons of stone had been despatched annually in the early years of the century. A staff of one sufficed after 1913. (M.Dart)

ELBURTON CROSS

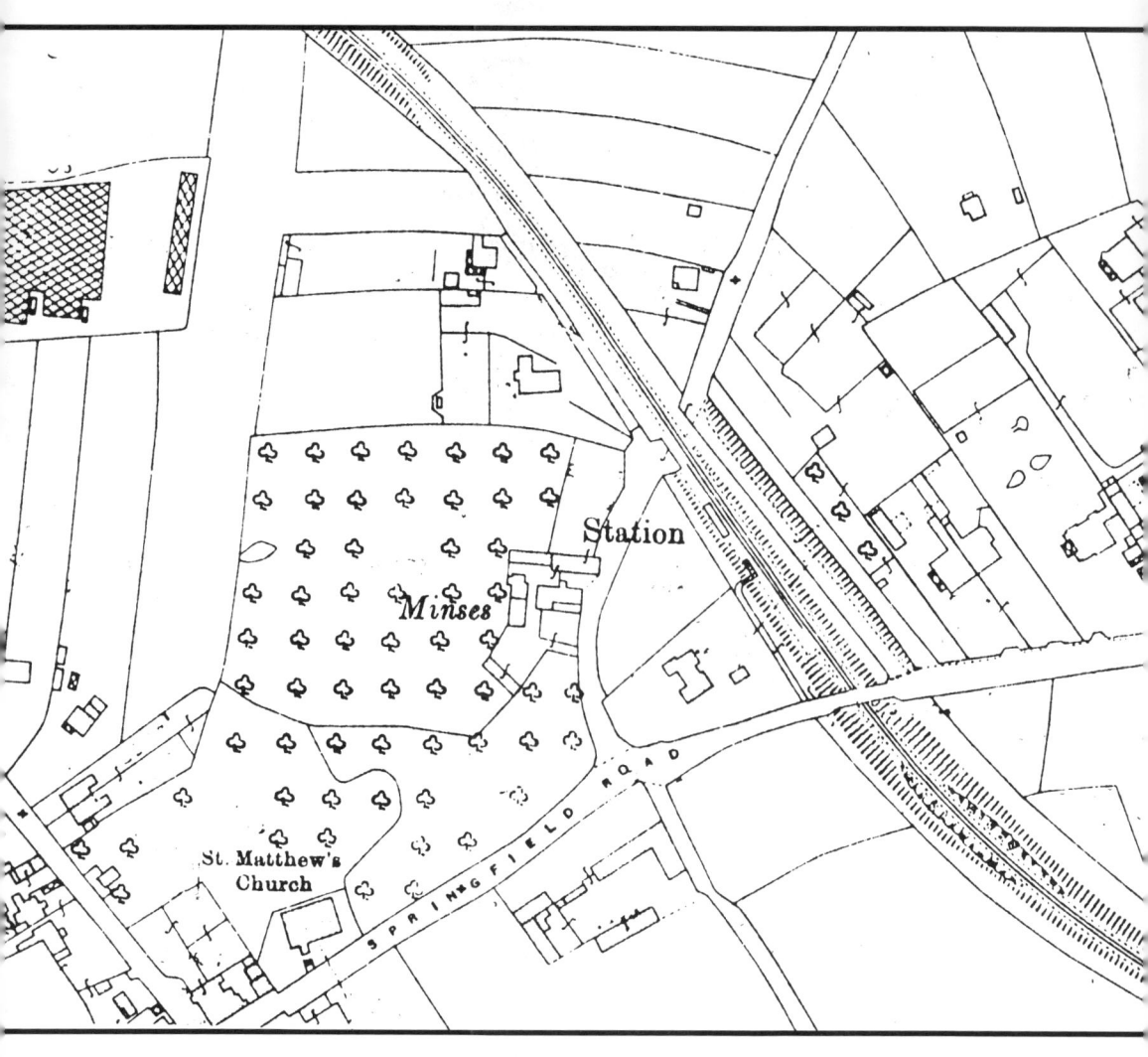

XXVI The 1933 survey indicates that the station was situated between an overbridge and an underbridge. One man was employed here until 1930.

ELBURTON CROSS	1903	1913	1923
Passenger tickets issued	11355	20831	17836
Season tickets issued	*	*	196
Parcels forwarded	-	2298	1962
General goods forwarded (tons)			
Coal and coke received (tons)			
Other minerals received (tons)			
General goods received (tons)			
Trucks of livestock handled			

110. The Plymouth Railway Circle's special on 27th February 1960 was hauled by 2-6-2T no. 4549 and stopped for members to examine the remains of the station, notably the steps on the side of the cutting. No trace now remains. (M.Dart)

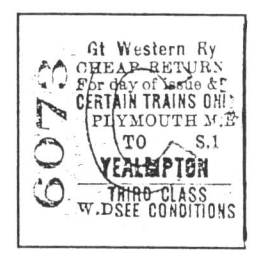

BRIXTON ROAD

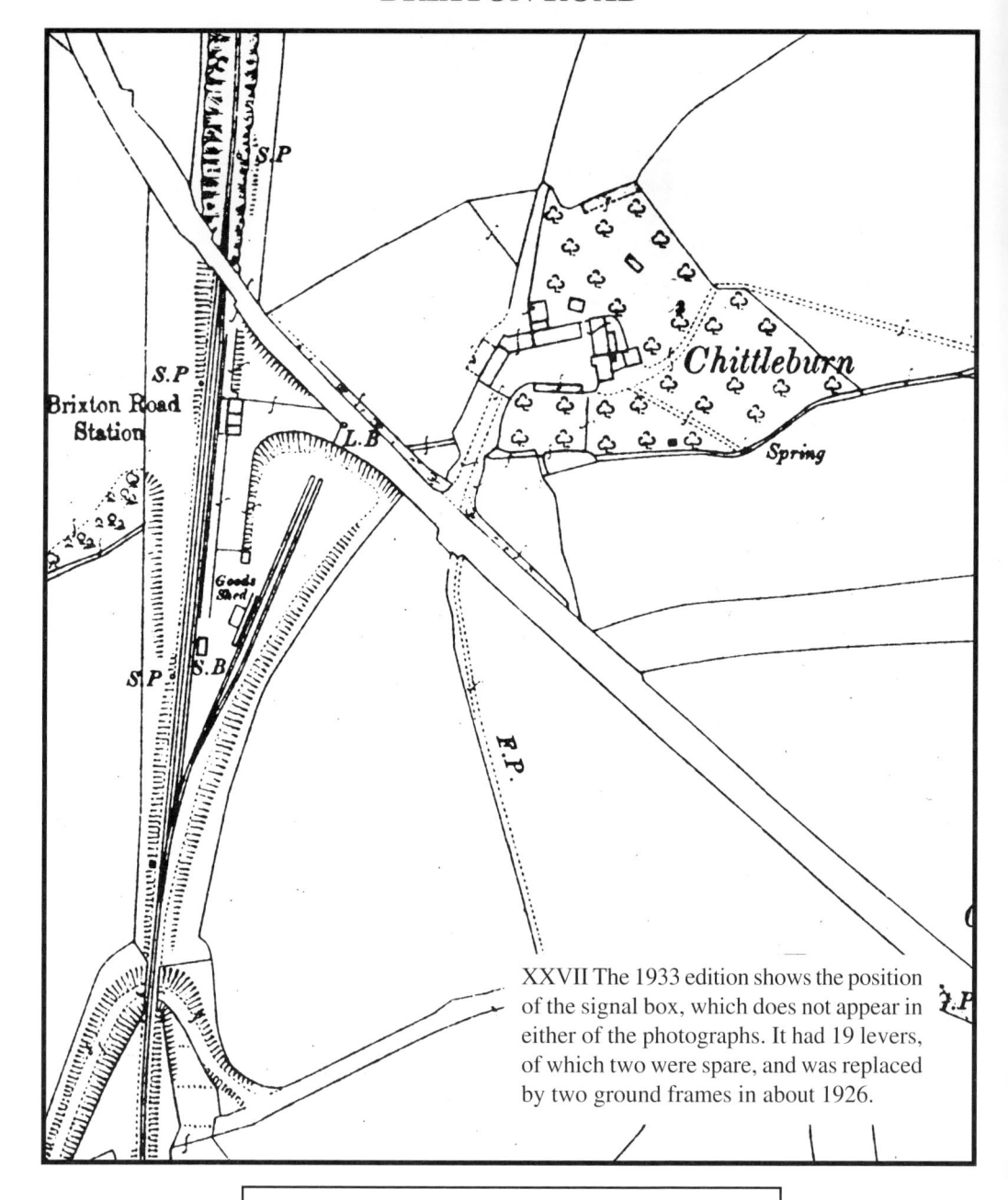

XXVII The 1933 edition shows the position of the signal box, which does not appear in either of the photographs. It had 19 levers, of which two were spare, and was replaced by two ground frames in about 1926.

BRIXTON ROAD	1903	1913	1923	1933
Passenger tickets issued	10430	10720	8712	
Season tickets issued	*	*	53	
Parcels forwarded	1817	1982	679	
General goods forwarded (tons)	32	54	17	7
Coal and coke received (tons)	396	352	153	59
Other minerals received (tons)	1146	828	979	11
General goods received (tons)	57	77	85	7
Trucks of livestock handled	-	-	1	-

111. Taken soon after the opening, this view would have later included two semaphore signals, one near the road bridge and one in the foreground. Horses had to have patience as one of their features. (British Rail)

112. The REC Railtour in April 1959 waits while photographers record that the architecture (and even the timber addition) was similar to that at Billacombe and also Yealmpton. However, the building still stands today, much enlarged and in residential use. (A.E.Bennett)

STEER POINT

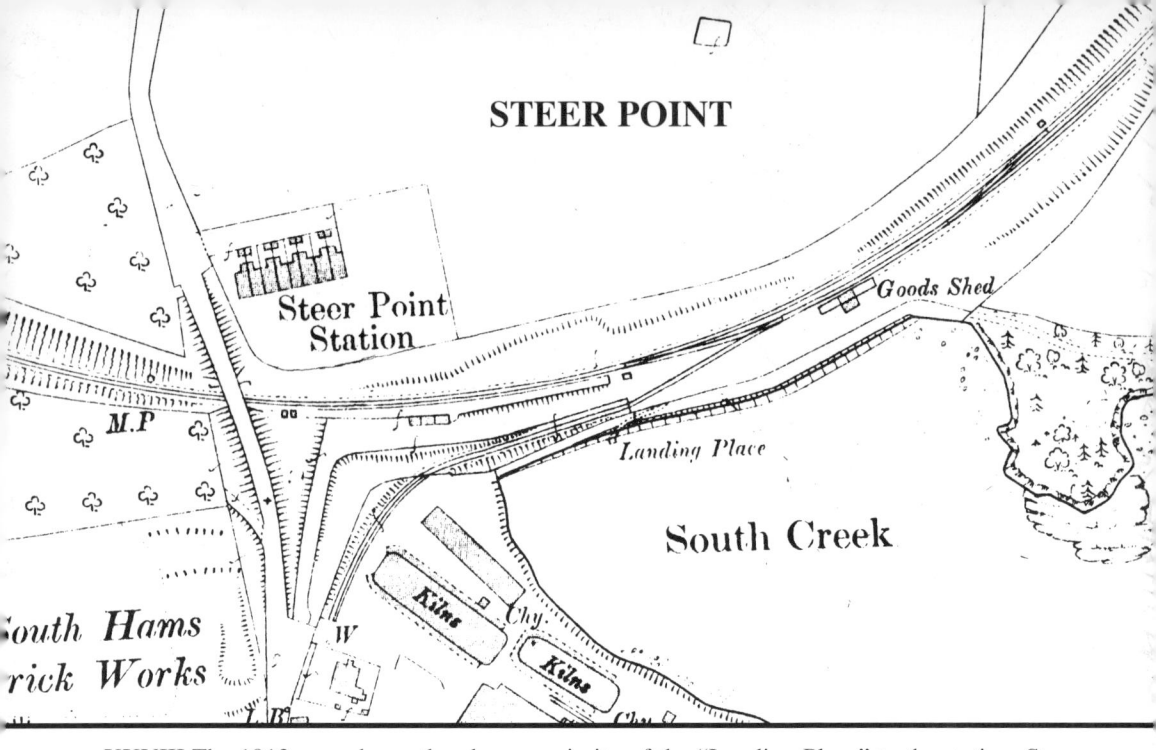

XXVIII The 1913 map shows the close proximity of the "Landing Place" to the station. Steamers operated from here to Newton Ferrers and Noss Mayo; these were used by daily passengers to and from Plymouth. There was no signalling at this location. The nearby brickworks accounted for much of the "coal inward" and "mineral outward".

113. The small goods shed is in the distance as a steam railcar arrives with a coach in tow in about 1928. Oyster traffic once contributed to the large number of "parcels despatched". This was the only building to be reused again in 1941-47; it was clad with corrugated iron. Only the platform edge survived into the 1990s.
(Lens of Sutton)

STEER POINT	1903	1913	1923	1933
Passenger tickets issued	12249	15739	11867	
Season tickets issued	*	*	94	
Parcels forwarded	1386	3780	1719	
General goods forwarded (tons)	6	78	17	26
Coal and coke received (tons)	2092	2236	497	1416
Other minerals received (tons)	663	36	88	26
General goods received (tons)	82	145	38	102
Trucks of livestock handled	-	-	-	-

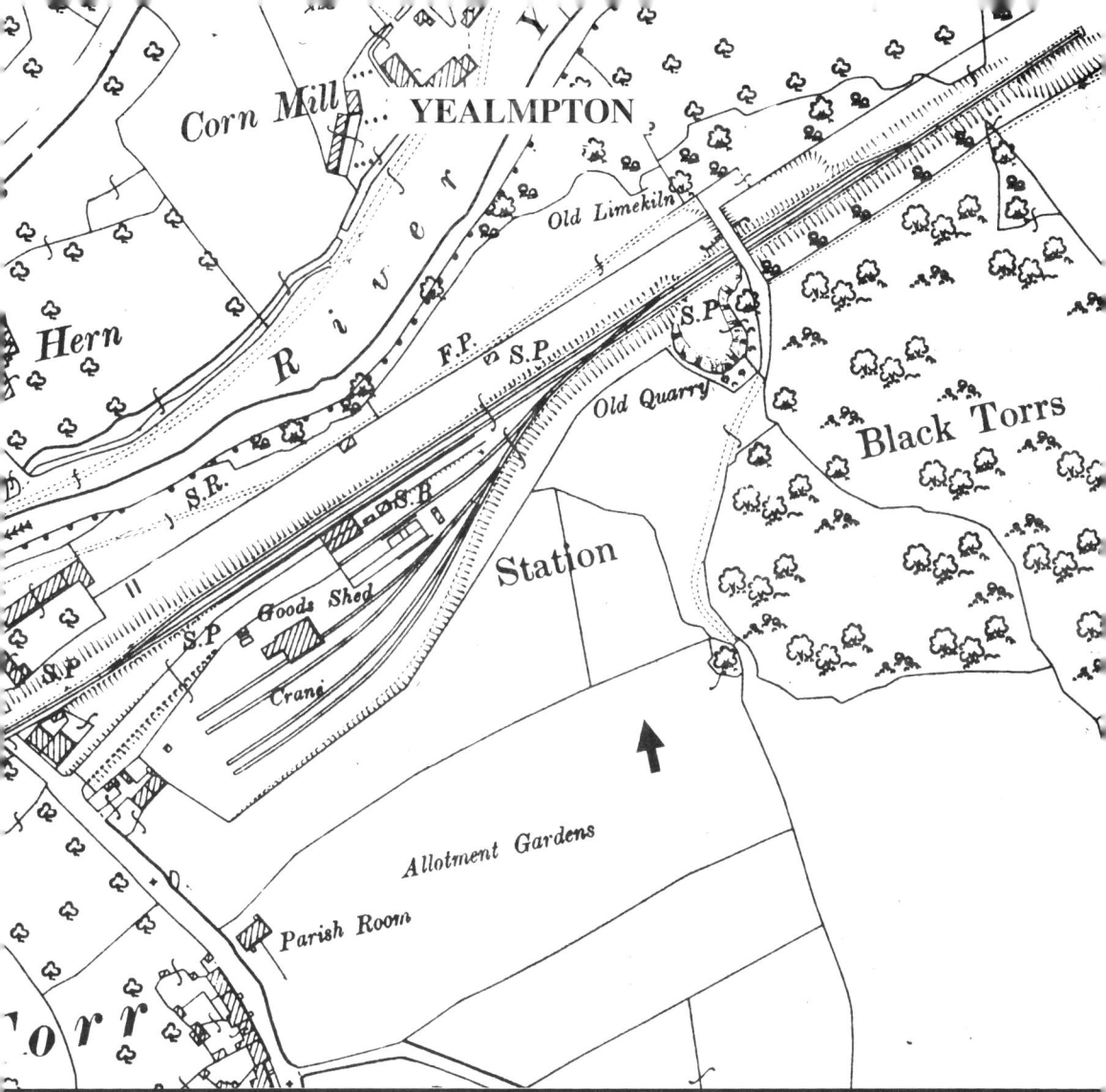

XXIX The end of the branch is featured on the 1906 edition, the layout being unchanged throughout the life of the line. The crane shown was of only 30 cwt capacity. The water tank was close to the River Yealm. The proposed extension to Modbury is on the right.

YEALMPTOM	1903	1913	1923	1933
Passenger tickets issued	2164	55798	21909	
Season tickets issued	*	*	216	
Parcels forwarded	10426	15093	7906	
General goods forwarded (tons)	386	427	253	222
Coal and coke received (tons)	1663	2280	1027	2276
Other minerals received (tons)	1749	3200	2187	354
General goods received (tons)	671	2374	1105	1591
Trucks of livestock handled	158	229	95	38

114. A class 1901 0-6-0ST waits to depart for Millbay before the days of push-pull working. Lighting by oil was standard at rural stations. Four lamps are visible and there are two in the next view. (M.Dart coll.)

115. Part of the long loop is evident as a train approaches the terminus. The signal box was in use until 23rd January 1931, when three ground frames were installed. Staff was cut from five to one in 1930. (Lens of Sutton)

116. The connecting bus to Bigbury-on-Sea waits in the station approach. By 1926, a GWR bus left Millbay at 10am and 6pm and took passengers direct without change in 1 hour 45 minutes. The once familiar GWR official document box awaits loading. (M.Dart coll.)

117. No. 4693 creeps into one of the sidings to collect condemned coaches on 20th June 1950, while others (right) stand in the platform. For many years, the goods train departed from Laira Yard at 11.30am and was due back at 4.40pm. (J.J.Smith)

118. The goods shed and cattle pen were recorded on the same day. The toilet block (right) was added in 1941, as the station building was let out as a dwelling. (J.J.Smith)

119. The RCTS special train on 2nd May 1959 was composed of four autocoaches, with 0-6-0PT no. 6420 in the centre. The platform was partly occupied by a wooden extension of the type seen in pictures 107 and 112. (S.C.Nash)

120. The exterior was photographed on the same day. The "Pagoda" had been erected in 1941 to serve as a ticket office. The site was cleared in November 1971 to make way for over 30 houses, which now stand in Riverside Walk. (R.M.Casserley)

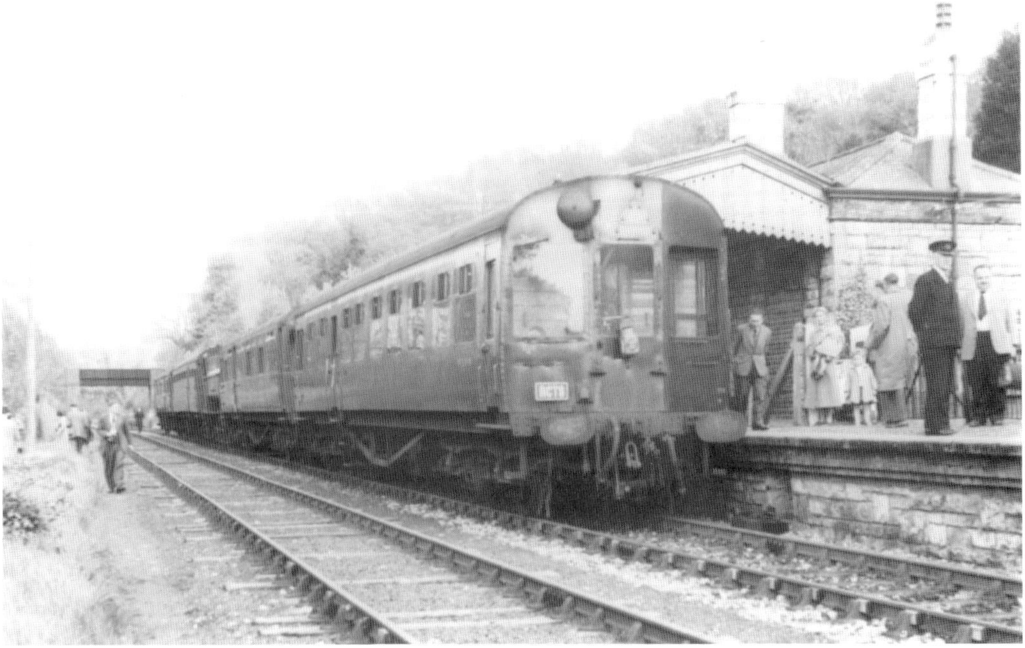

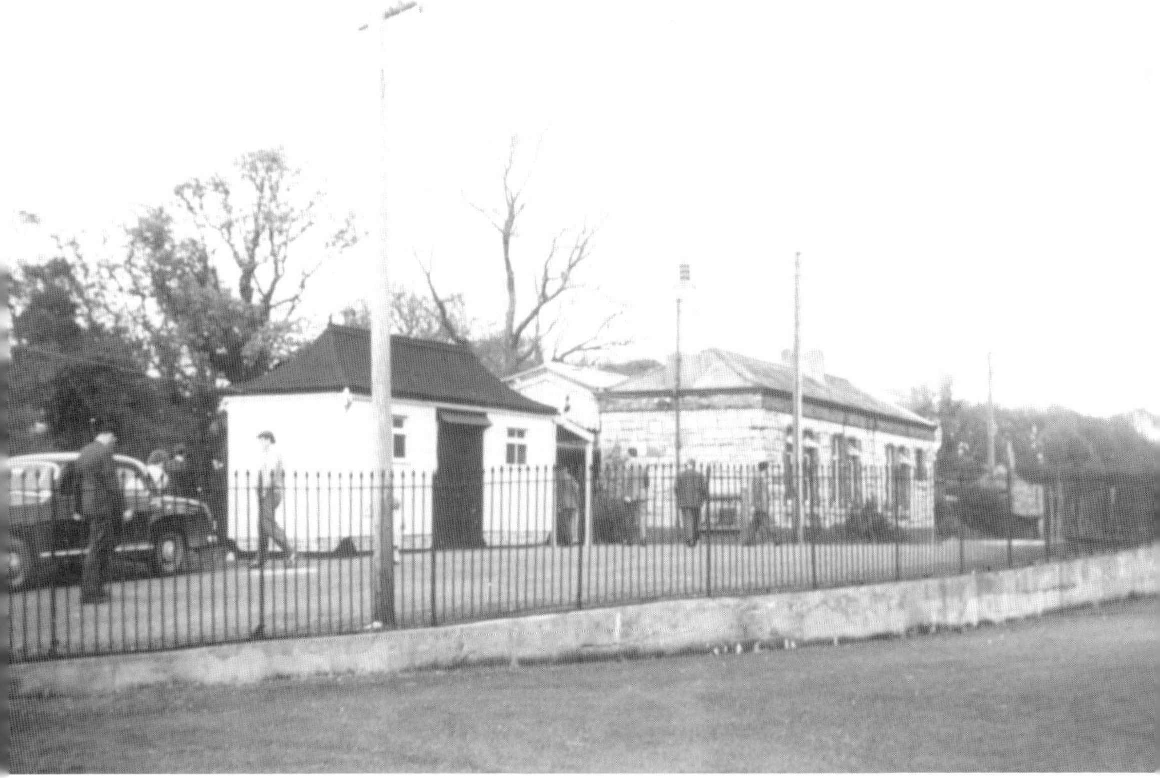

MP Middleton Press

Easebourne Lane, Midhurst, W Sussex. GU29 9AZ Tel: 01730 813169 Fax: 01730 812601
Email: sales@middletonpress.co.uk   www.middletonpress.co.uk
If books are not available from your local transport stockist, order direct post free UK.

BRANCH LINES
Branch Line to Allhallows
Branch Line to Alton
Branch Lines around Ascot
Branch Line to Ashburton
Branch Lines around Bodmin
Branch Line to Bude
Branch Lines around Canterbury
Branch Lines around Chard & Yeovil
Branch Line to Cheddar
Branch Lines around Cromer
Branch Line to the Derwent Valley
Branch Lines to East Grinstead
Branch Lines of East London
Branch Lines to Effingham Junction
Branch Lines to Enfield Town & Palace Gates
Branch Lines to Falmouth, Helston & St. Ives
Branch Line to Fairford
Branch Lines to Felixstowe & Aldeburgh
Branch Lines around Gosport
Branch Line to Hayling
Branch Lines to Henley, Windsor & Marlow
Branch Line to Hawkhurst
Branch Line to Horsham
Branch Lines around Huntingdon
Branch Line to Ilfracombe
Branch Line to Kingsbridge
Branch Line to Kingswear
Branch Line to Lambourn
Branch Lines to Launceston & Princetown
Branch Lines to Longmoor
Branch Line to Looe
Branch Line to Lyme Regis
Branch Line to Lynton
Branch Lines around March
Branch Lines around Midhurst
Branch Line to Minehead
Branch Line to Moretonhampstead
Branch Lines to Newport (IOW)
Branch Lines to Newquay
Branch Lines around North Woolwich
Branch Line to Padstow
Branch Lines around Plymouth
Branch Lines to Princes Risborough
Branch Lines to Seaton and Sidmouth
Branch Lines around Sheerness
Branch Line to Shrewsbury
Branch Line to Tenterden
Branch Lines around Tiverton
Branch Lines to Torrington
Branch Lines to Tunbridge Wells
Branch Line to Upwell
Branch Line to Wantage (The Wantage Tramway)
Branch Lines of West London
Branch Lines of West Wiltshire
Branch Lines around Weymouth
Branch Lines around Wimborne
Branch Lines around Wisbech

NARROW GAUGE
Austrian Narrow Gauge
Branch Line to Lynton
Branch Lines around Portmadoc 1923-46
Branch Lines around Porthmadog 1954-94
Branch Line to Southwold
Douglas to Port Erin
Douglas to Peel
Hampshire Narrow Gauge
Kent Narrow Gauge
Northern France Narrow Gauge
Romneyrail
Sierra Leone Narrow Gauge
Southern France Narrow Gauge
Sussex Narrow Gauge
Surrey Narrow Gauge
Swiss Narrow Gauge
Two-Foot Gauge Survivors
Vivarais Narrow Gauge

SOUTH COAST RAILWAYS
Ashford to Dover
Bournemouth to Weymouth
Brighton to Eastbourne
Brighton to Worthing
Dover to Ramsgate
Eastbourne to Hastings
Hastings to Ashford
Ryde to Ventnor
Southampton to Bournemouth

SOUTHERN MAIN LINES
Basingstoke to Salisbury
Crawley to Littlehampton
Dartford to Sittingbourne
East Croydon to Three Bridges
Epsom to Horsham
Exeter to Barnstaple
Exeter to Tavistock
London Bridge to East Croydon
Tonbridge to Hastings
Salisbury to Yeovil
Sittingbourne to Ramsgate
Swanley to Ashford
Tavistock to Plymouth
Three Bridges to Brighton
Victoria to Bromley South
Victoria to East Croydon
Waterloo to Windsor
Waterloo to Woking
Woking to Portsmouth
Woking to Southampton
Yeovil to Exeter

EASTERN MAIN LINES
Barking to Southend
Ely to Kings Lynn
Ely to Norwich
Fenchurch Street to Barking
Hitchin to Peterborough
Ilford to Shenfield
Ipswich to Saxmundham
Liverpool Street to Ilford
Saxmundham to Yarmouth
Tilbury Loop

WESTERN MAIN LINES
Banbury to Birmingham
Bristol to Taunton
Didcot to Banbury
Didcot to Swindon
Ealing to Slough
Exeter to Newton Abbot
Moreton-in-Marsh to Worcester
Newton Abbot to Plymouth
Newbury to Westbury
Oxford to Moreton-in-Marsh
Paddington to Ealing
Paddington to Princes Risborough
Plymouth to St. Austell
Princes Risborough to Banbury
Reading to Didcot
Slough to Newbury
St. Austell to Penzance
Swindon to Bristol
Swindon to Newport
Taunton to Exeter
Westbury to Taunton

MIDLAND MAIN LINES
Bedford to Wellingborough
Euston to Harrow & Wealdstone
Gloucester to Bristol
Harrow to Watford
St. Albans to Bedford
St. Pancras to St. Albans

COUNTRY RAILWAY ROUTES
Abergavenny to Merthyr
Andover to Southampton
Bath to Evercreech Junction
Bath Green Park to Bristol
Bournemouth to Evercreech Junction
Brecon to Newport
Burnham to Evercreech Junction
Cheltenham to Andover
Croydon to East Grinstead
Didcot to Winchester
East Kent Light Railway
Fareham to Salisbury
Frome to Bristol
Guildford to Redhill
Reading to Basingstoke
Reading to Guildford
Redhill to Ashford
Salisbury to Westbury
Stratford upon Avon to Cheltenham
Strood to Paddock Wood
Taunton to Barnstaple
Wenford Bridge to Fowey
Westbury to Bath
Woking to Alton
Yeovil to Dorchester

GREAT RAILWAY ERAS
Ashford from Steam to Eurostar
Festiniog in the Fifties
Festiniog in the Sixties
Festiniog 50 years of enterprise
Isle of Wight Lines 50 years of change
Railways to Victory 1944-46
Return to Blaenau 1970-82
SECR Centenary album
Talyllyn 50 years of change
Wareham to Swanage 50 years of change
Yeovil 50 years of change

LONDON SUBURBAN RLYS
Caterham and Tattenham Corner
Charing Cross to Dartford
Clapham Jn. to Beckenham Jn.
Crystal Palace (HL) & Catford Loop
East London Line
Finsbury Park to Alexandra Palace
Holborn Viaduct to Lewisham
Kingston and Hounslow Loops
Lewisham to Dartford
Lines around Wimbledon
Liverpool Street to Chingford
Mitcham Junction Lines
North London Line
South London Line
West Croydon to Epsom
West London Line
Willesden Junction to Richmond
Wimbledon to Beckenham
Wimbledon to Epsom

STEAMING THROUGH
Steaming through Cornwall
Steaming through the Isle of Wight
Steaming through Kent
Steaming through West Hants

TRAMWAY CLASSICS
Aldgate & Stepney Tramways
Barnet & Finchley Tramways
Bath Tramways
Brighton's Tramways
Bristol's Tramways
Burton & Ashby Tramways
Camberwell & W.Norwood Tramways
Chesterfield Tramways
Clapham & Streatham Tramways
Croydon's Tramways
Derby Tramways
Dover's Tramways
East Ham & West Ham Tramways
Edgware and Willesden Tramways
Eltham & Woolwich Tramways
Embankment & Waterloo Tramways
Exeter & Taunton Tramways
Fulwell - Home to Trams, Trolleys and Buses
Great Yarmouth Tramways
Greenwich & Dartford Tramways
Hammersmith & Hounslow Tramways
Hampstead & Highgate Tramways
Holborn & Finsbury Tramways
Ilford & Barking Tramways
Kingston & Wimbledon Tramways
Lewisham & Catford Tramways
Liverpool Tramways 1. Eastern Routes
Liverpool Tramways 2. Southern Routes
Liverpool Tramways 3. Northern Routes
Maidstone & Chatham Tramways
Margate to Ramsgate
North Kent Tramways
Norwich Tramways
Reading Tramways
Shepherds Bush & Uxbridge Tramways
Southend-on-sea Tramways
South London Line Tramways 1903-33
Southwark & Deptford Tramways
Stamford Hill Tramways
Twickenham & Kingston Tramways
Victoria & Lambeth Tramways
Waltham Cross & Edmonton Tramways
Walthamstow & Leyton Tramways
Wandsworth & Battersea Tramways

TROLLEYBUS CLASSICS
Bradford Trolleybuses
Croydon Trolleybuses
Darlington Trolleybuses
Derby Trolleybuses
Huddersfield Trolleybuses
Hull Trolleybuses
Portsmouth Trolleybuses
Reading Trolleybuses

WATERWAY & SHIPPING
Kent and East Sussex Waterways
London to Portsmouth Waterways
Sussex Shipping - Sail, Steam & Motor
West Sussex Waterways

MILITARY BOOKS
Battle over Portsmouth
Battle over Sussex 1940
Blitz over Sussex 1941-42
Bombers over Sussex 1943-45
Bognor at War
East Ridings Secret Resistance
Military Defence of West Sussex
Military Signals from the South Coast
Secret Sussex Resistance
Sussex Home Guard
Surrey Home Guard

OTHER RAILWAY BOOKS
Collectors for Trains, Trolleys & Trams
Industrial Railways of the South-East
South Eastern & Chatham Railways
London Chatham & Dover Railway
London Termini - Past and Proposed
War on the Line (SR 1939-45)